What people are saying about

Building Your Financial Portfolio On $25 A Month

"Simply the best investment book yet!! Extremely practical." (On-The-Money, financial book review)

"Excellent! . . . interesting and enjoyable . . . great information." (Linda Neilson, Bronx, NY)

"...recommending it to everyone I know..." (Doris Gagnon, Overland Park, KS)

"...concise, clear, and very informative." (Sharon & John Curry, Independence, MO)

"A wealth of information! A must take seminar for the small investor." (Phyllis Durr, Washington, DC)

"Our most popular class..." (Communiversity, University of Missouri, Kansas City, MO)

"Your advice was simple and honest...it's as easy as you described." (Michelle de Jesus, San Francisco, CA)

Adding To Your Financial Portfolio

"...so simple it's actually enjoyable...investing really is for everyone..." (Manny Carbahal, CPA, Davis, CA)

"...fascinating and edifying...extremely helpful...clear, concise, well-reasoned..." (Marion, Librarian, Culver City, CA)

The Banker Chronicles (mystery)

"Couldn't put it down." (Sharon Curry, Independence, MO)

"It was great! I love the story." (Darlene Schrag, Chicago, IL)

Building Your Dream Life: Career, Sex & Leisure

"...positive, powerful and packed with good ideas for success in life and in business...clearly written, delightfully easy to read...practical and attainable advice..." (Sacramento Public Library)

SMART REAL ESTATE INVESTING
© 2007

Bobbie Christensen
Eric Christensen

EFFECTIVE LIVING PUBLISHING
P. O. Box 232233
Sacramento, CA 95823
ELPBooks@aol.com

SMART REAL ESTATE INVESTING
Published by Effective Living Publishing
P. O. Box 232233, Sacramento, CA 95823
(916) 422-8435; orders (800) 929-7889
Email: ELPBooks@aol.com
Website: www.BooksAmerica.com

Cover design by Mustang Graphic Designers,
mustanggraphic@aol.com

ISBN: 0972917365

TABLE OF CONTENTS

SAFETY VS. RISK

The common perception of investing in real estate today is that it is easy, safe and you will become rich in a very short time. But perception is not truth.

The facts are: Investing in real estate varies from quite time consuming to extremely time consuming. As the price of property varies from low to high depending on the local and national economy, it is only safe over a long period of time and even that is not guaranteed. It is not a liquid asset in that it can take a very long time to sell this type of investment. Most people who claim to be rich from investing in real estate are only rich on paper in that they own a lot of property. But, again, turning this paper wealth into money you can actually use can take a long period of time and is not guaranteed because you are always subject to things such as location, time of year, and the local economy.

However, if you find real estate so interesting that you are willing to spend hours a week working in it and are interested in building a good amount of equity and/or you want a good monthly income, then real estate may be for you.

There are a lot of books and seminars out there making ludicrous and/or exaggerated claims. There is the one about buying real estate with no money down. This can be done but it is very difficult because you need excellent, as in perfect, credit or a property owner is willing to deal directly with you and require no money down because something is very wrong and they have to get rid of that property quickly. There are even some classes suggesting real estate as a good way to hide money from the IRS (not suggested unless you want to handle your investments from prison which is also illegal). Never fool with the IRS! It is not worth it. There are also the ads for computer software that will calculate and figure everything out for you. No software can help you with any type of investing because investing is not a science with exact numbers and details.

This book is how to invest in real estate so as to make money rather than lose money. In other words, *smart* investing.

It is much more time consuming and riskier then the stock market investing we recommend in our book *"Building Your Financial Portfolio On $25 A Month (Or Less)"*. However, from our nationwide seminars on this subject, we realize that many people are interested in real estate. Our purpose with this book is to make sure you do it the safest way possible, the way we do it ourselves. We cannot guarantee huge profits as we don't have a crystal ball that looks into the future, but we can promise good profits or a good monthly retirement income if you make wise informed decisions. You can also minimize any potential risk by becoming better informed and spending the necessary time to learn about the market and your area. The more time you put into becoming knowledgeable about real estate and the market you are interested in, the higher your chances are of being successful and with less risk.

Investing in real estate can help you financially because it is a tangible asset meaning that property is a real thing that you control, you can make money from either through the building of equity and/or through rental income, plus it has tax advantages. Although real estate is not as volatile as the stock market, it is also not any where near as liquid as you cannot sell it overnight when necessary. But for the long-term investor who finds real estate so interesting that you are willing to spend the extensive time necessary, it can add to your wealth and you can make it grow for you.

This book is set up by type of real estate investing so that you can easily decide which type is best for you and then follow the advice for that particular type of investing. Each section will cover a different type of real estate investing and will include what is involved time and money wise, how to find the financing, finding a good deal, negotiating the purchase, building equity in your investment, and how to make money either through renting the property or through selling it at a profit.

The idea behind investing in real estate is to put as little money down as possible so you are using someone else's money (the lender's) and then create as much equity as you can through renovations and through the growth of the housing market. However, the home you will live in and raise your family in is also an investment. As such and in order to live comfortably, you will want to put as much of your own money into the down payment as you can to keep your monthly mortgage payment lower. We will be concentrating on other forms of investing wherein you can make money either very quickly (as in rental income) or over a longer period of time (as in fix it up and then sell for

3

a profit). Keep in mind that many of the different ways of building equity will still apply to your own home.

Either way, you need to make an informed decision and a good business decision or you could end up with a large financial problem.

Kathy bought a house near a college campus with the intention of renting it to a co-ed who would rent out the other bedrooms to students. But just as she closed on the mortgage, Kathy found rental rates dropping due to a developing recession and a large surplus of rental property available in her area. She was left with a house she could not get her monthly mortgage payment back on to say nothing of covering the taxes. On top of that, she found the house needed major repairs she had not foreseen. What was supposed to be a little extra rental income for Kathy was quickly becoming a money hog. And because she could not afford the necessary repairs, Kathy was spending every spare minute trying to correct things herself. She quickly discovered that maintenance was not her calling in life.

Let's make sure this type of thing does not happen to you and your investment. The first way is to make sure you are investing in something you enjoy. If you enjoy doing something, it will be much easier to carry through and do the necessary work.

WHAT TYPE OF REAL ESTATE INVESTMENT IS RIGHT FOR YOU

We are firm believers that everyone should do the things they like to do. Obviously there are times when you have to do things you don't want to do but that doesn't mean you can't spend the majority of your time involved in interesting exciting activities. Therefore, before deciding to jump into real estate investing, you need to make sure it is the right thing for you. Otherwise, you can waste a lot of money on an expensive mistake.

To be successful you need to have self-confidence, be detail oriented. You must like solving problems, have persistence, and be organized. However, do not think you have to be perfect. If you are not particularly organized or too impatient or whatever, is there someone else in your life that does have the traits you are lacking that you could work well with? After all, no one is perfect! However, we did have one class wherein a woman claimed she was perfect in everything (a very difficult class to teach). You will also have help with some things as you will be dealing with a real estate agent, inspectors, lenders, and others. This idea of sharing what one lacks is probably why we have been married for over 30 years. However, keep in mind when working with someone else that only one person can be the final decision maker. Someone has to take charge or no decisions will ever be made.

It also helps to decide up front if you are looking for fast profits, long-term appreciation in value, and/or income. However, remember that fast profits also means much more risk while long-term appreciation and income are the safer investments.

There are many different kinds of real estate investing but only a few that we feel are the safest. If you want to know how to risk everything you own, just read someone else's book! We have also covered some investment possibilities that we would never personally recommend in the final chapter. Keep in mind that investing in your own home is the biggest investment most people will ever make. It might be your one and only home or you might start with a fixer-upper and then use that to build equity and slowly climb the property ladder to that big dream house. As always, our belief is that you should invest in things that are as safe as possible. If you really want to risk everything, go to Las Vegas!

So what are the different possibilities for investing in real estate?

Your Own Home

Buying your own home is usually the biggest investment any family ever makes (because it costs so much!). It is where you will be spending most of your relaxing off-work hours, where you will raise a family, where you will be involved in your hobbies and interests, and the place that will be the backdrop for many, many memories. However, because it does involve so much of your hard earned money, you need to be logical about it (think with your head and not your heart). Therefore, you

6

need to think about how much you can afford and what is the best location for you. Although you need to buy a home where you will be working, there are many different locations in that area to consider. Investing in your home can help you in many ways in the future also.

Fix and Flip House

This is where you buy property for a low or below market price because it needs some (or a great deal of) renovating. You do the fixing up and then sell it for a good profit. This can all be done in from one month to one year depending on how much time and money you have to put into it.

Usually the idea is to buy, fix, and sell quickly. The longer it takes to sell, the longer you will be paying that monthly mortgage and insurance out of your pocket. The secret to making a quick profit like this is to plan, plan, plan!

To maximize your profit you are looking for a property that needs a lot of fixing and you can, therefore, buy it for a reasonable price. That is the first part. Then come the difficult parts of fixing it up and selling it.

Having personally renovated everything from newer homes that just needed a little updating and painting to tearing out walls in a 100 year old house and rebuilding from the frame out, we feel this is a young person's game because of the intensive physical labor involved. You also need to like and want to learn the necessary skills such as painting, sheet rocking, electrical and general carpentry. If you already have some experience with these things, you will be able to fix and flip much faster then someone who has to learn all these things from scratch. We did it when we were younger and made very good profits. So you need to ask yourself, "have I got the hundreds of hours and the strength and the no-how to do this kind of work?" Otherwise, you can hire people to do some or even all of the work for you, but you will be cutting into your profits drastically and could even end up without a profit. Remember, the more you can actually do yourself, the better your profit will be. There is a reason why it is called "sweat equity".

You can build your real estate portfolio by then using the profit from this first house to buy more fix and flip property.

Apartment Rental Property

In this, you may buy a property that has 1, 2, 3 or more units in perfect condition or one that needs some work. Obviously you will get a better deal with a higher profit upon selling the property if you look for a building that needs any where from some to a lot of renovation. You do the repair work and any other renovations necessary and then rent out each unit for a monthly income that, hopefully, covers all the mortgage costs (plus taxes, maintenance, insurance, etc.) for additional income. You can add to this one property with more property and create a complete monthly income for you if you like.

The part we like about this is that you are doing everything you did with a fix and flip but you have more time because you can actually live in one of the units while you are fixing it up, therefore, making this a long term project. Some day you will sell the property but, for rental purposes, this is not a concern in the purchasing of the property as you will be making a monthly income from it. However, you can also use the ever increasing equity (through appreciation as well as increasing rental) to finance the purchase of another rental property.

Family House Rental

In this case, you are buying a house and usually living in it while you fix it up. However, instead of selling the property for a profit, you use the equity to purchase another house and rent out this property you have fixed up. The advantages to this are that you have longer to do the fixing because you are also using it as your living quarters in the meantime and you can fix it up depending on your time schedule and abilities while spacing out the costs of your improvements. However, what if you like where you are living and do not want to move?

You could simply use the equity (or increased value) of this house to buy another one that you will rent to a family or to a group. Obviously, you would need to either buy something in good condition now or plan on a certain amount of time and money to fix it up for rental. Again, the idea is to build your real estate portfolio by buying more and more property that will grow in value, give you tax benefits, and create monthly income for you.

Vacation Property Rental

This varies from the above in that you will find a particular location that people (including yourself) like to vacation in. You could buy a very nice property or it could involve some fixing before you can rent it out. This gives you a vacation place along with rental income.

The down side is that it is usually more difficult to keep a vacation rental filled all season meaning you will have to cover the costs when it is not rented. Actually, the rental income will only help you cover some of the costs. However, if this is a place you and your family really love to visit, you also need to consider how much you would spend on going there each year and renting a place to stay in.

Vacation property is usually beside or near water such as the ocean, lake or river. These seem to be the easiest to rent. However, some people like the mountains for skiing in the winter but you can still rent it out in the summer if it is near a body of water. You will find in the chapter pertaining to vacation rentals that we have also included other vacation "things" you can rent out such as an RV or a boat.

Commercial Rental

If the entire building (which can be a converted house) is commercial rental space, your rental income will be higher. The turn over rate will depend on who you are renting to. A doctor, optometrist, or other professional will usually stay in the same location for many years. However, restaurants and specialty stores come and go very quickly. The much higher rental you can get from these types of properties can quickly be offset by very long periods of your paying for empty space while you look for a new tenant. Buying a property that has room for more than one commercial rental will help in that you should have at least one other unit rented out while you are looking to fill that empty spot.

Also, usually you are responsible for any renovations needed in order for the unit to fit what the new tenant needs. That is, a doctor's office would need a very different setup from a restaurant. This can be a huge added expense for you.

It is very difficult to find commercial rental space at a good price because everything available has been bought up by investment companies specializing in this sort of thing. Obviously it is much easier and more affordable to find a house that can be converted to office space. The rental for office space is much higher then for apartment space, however, the risk is higher in that you need to think of renovations for a new client, plenty of parking, long periods of empty space, and, most importantly, can you even get the variances and permits required to change this house into a business location. Check out the variance and permit situation first before even making a bid on such property.

Mixed Use Property – Buying a building, usually in a downtown area, can sometimes be used for commercial rental as well as living rental. That is, the street level floor is rented to a business such as a restaurant or store with living apartments on the above floors. Again, this gives you rental income but the commercial area will bring in a much higher rental income.

This can be a better situation than the above commercial rental in that, even when that street level area

11

is vacant, you still have the apartment rental to help covers the bills.

However, you still need to find out about getting a variance to change from a residential to commercial unit. Again, you need to think about costly renovations and plenty of parking.

Other Real Estate Investments such as REITs – You can invest in real estate without actually being involved in it in several ways. As opposed to investing in individual types of property, with REITs you would be using your money but not have to use your time or work effort. However, these can be very risky. We have reserved one chapter for risky investments that we would personally never get involved in and why.

* * * * *

We want to repeat that there are many other ways to invest in real estate but we will not recommend methods that we would not do ourselves. If you have read any of our previous books or attended our classes, you know that we do not want to see you risking your own or your family's future on risky ventures. And why bother with risk when you there are plenty of safer opportunities?

Which one is right for you? We will cover in detail what is involved in each of these in following chapters. However, the most important thing you need to know in order to be successful at any of these situations is "how organized are you?"

You must be organized as you will be either doing a lot of work yourself or hiring people to do the work for you or, if you are really lucky, you are working with a spouse or partner who is good at the things you are not. After all, no one is good at everything so you need to know what your strong points are and then find others who are good at the things you are not. You may love fixing a place up yourself with all the painting and choosing carpeting, but what about the clean up part? If you positively cannot force yourself to do the cleaning, is your partner going to do it or will you have to hire someone to do this part for you? Again, anything you have to have hired help for is going to cut into your profits.

You also have others that can help you. Us! We are here to help you with some things you may not be good at such as finding the money, making smart decisions, and getting organized!

Keep in mind that we strongly suggest you keep your risk to a minimum which means only investing as much money as you can live without for at least 3 to 5 years. You may make your profit sooner then that but even a fix and flip deal that was supposed to provide you a profit in just a couple of months can end up taking several years.

Making a profit from any real estate can take different forms. If you will be renting out property, your rental income should cover the following ongoing costs:
    monthly mortgage payment
    taxes
    insurance
    ongoing and occasional surprise maintenance

Having rental property will also help you in several ways besides just getting that monthly income.

Taxes - There are several tax advantages to owning property. Rental property can be depreciated on your taxes wherein a certain amount of what you paid is tax free each year until the property is fully depreciated. You can also deduct the interest on the mortgage, property taxes and any operating/maintenance costs from your taxes. In certain situations such as an historic building or a low-income rental building, you can get tax credits. Keep in mind that, after you retire, rental income does not take away from your social security benefits as other earned income will. You will find more on all of this in the following chapters.

Appreciation – Other than fix and flip property, you should think about the future appreciation you will build in this property. Even buying your own home creates appreciation. That is, as you pay off the mortgage, you will have more equity (value) in the property that can be used to finance the purchase of other property or used as collateral on loans for other purposes. This is appreciation that you have paid for.

There is also market appreciation as costs continue to rise. However, it is important to keep in mind that market appreciation is not a given as it was 20 years ago. Back then, if you bought any property it would increase in value whether you took care of it or not. This is not true today. Today it is not uncommon to see a property depreciate. It could be temporary due to an economic recession or it could be very long term due to a change in the neighborhood or due to neglect.

You can also increase the value of a home by updating it, adding to it, landscaping it, and in general keeping it in good condition.

Inflation and Recession – Periods of inflation whether nationwide or in your local area that are economic indicators or simply a rise in property values can be very useful to you. If the country goes into a period of inflation, the value of your property is going to increase and rentals will usually go up appropriately. If there is a localized inflation in property values, this will at least temporarily increase its value. This means that you can use this additional value for loans including financing more property or you can sell the property to get the actual money for it.

A recession can hurt you financially but, if you understand how to use it correctly, a period of economic recession can also help you. Just as with the stock market, if you can determine before others can that we are going into a period of recession, you can use this to your advantage (see *Adding To Your Financial Portfolio*). In a recession property prices drop. If you plan for this, you can pick up additional property (or your first piece of property) at a discount price. Also, usually in a recession not as many people can afford to buy a home and will thus be looking for a rental. This increase in renters can increase what you charge for monthly rental.

Interest rates on your mortgage are very much affected by inflation and recession. In inflation, the interest rates will be higher meaning more money you will have to pay each month. A recession will cause interest rates to drop meaning less out-of-pocket expense for you.

However, please keep in mind that we do not recommend balloon payments or floating interest rates for your mortgage as these can get you into a lot of trouble. We will explain this in detail in the section on financing your purchase

* * * * *

Keeping all these things in mind, is real estate investing for you? Only you can decide this. If you made your decision to continue, you now need to find a good deal. However, a good deal can vary from one type of property and location to another. Therefore, we will discuss each type separately.

However, before even looking at property to buy, you need to know whether you can afford to buy it. In other words, where is the money going to come from?

FINANCING YOUR PURCHASE

Before you start looking at property, you need to determine how you will finance the purchase. Unfortunately, too many people find the property they want and then try to find financing. Just as a car dealer is more than willing to find financing for your new car, your real estate agent will be more then willing to help you with financing your new property, but keep in mind that they may be getting kickbacks meaning you end up paying more then is necessary. You need to do the research on financing yourself and before you even start looking at any property to determine what you can afford.

Again, for a good investment, you want to use as little of your own money as possible. Therefore, you should be looking for a loan for 90% of the price with a 10% down payment.

Yes, you can find no-money-down opportunities but these are extremely rare and can be very risky. You could find someone selling a property that is willing to finance it for you. If so, you better find out WHY they are so anxious to sell quickly. Also, you need a very good lawyer to create a contract in your favor. You certainly don't want to suddenly find out that, if you are one day late with your payment (how dependable is the US postal system?), the seller has the right to take back the property and keep everything you have paid into it already. Also, when the seller is willing to finance the deal himself, he is usually asking a higher price then the going rate for that property, the loan will usually be for a shorter period of time than a standard 30 year mortgage, and the interest rate will be higher. In fact, the owner is probably asking too much for the property and thus no agent is willing to take it on. It could also be that, for reasons not obvious to the eye, no lender is willing to write a mortgage on the property. For instance, the bank may have found out that there is contaminated soil in the area, or no drinkable water, or that the area is prone to floods.

Rather than spending all your time trying to find a no-money-down situation, a much safer and less time consuming financing option is the usual lenders such as credit unions and banks. However, the rates and terms can vary tremendously so you will need to do your shopping. Check out your credit union, your bank, and other mortgage lenders. Your credit union will usually give you the best deal. Banks are the second best deal. You can check the prevailing rates online at Bankrate.com. The "other" mortgage lenders will usually have the worst deals. Keep in mind that you want to put as little of your own money into this as possible and you do not want to risk your financial security. Therefore, you are looking for a low interest rate and a small down payment and usually a 30 year term which will keep your payments lower than a shorter term. Just as important, you will also need to know what other fees are involved for that particular institution such as application fee, closing costs, title insurance, surveyor costs, bank appraiser, inspections, and possible legal fees. Keep in mind that a lender can offer a small interest rate and a small down payment if they are going to make more money from you on the miscellaneous things people usually forget to ask about such as fees and points (a point is 1% of the amount borrowed, 2 points is 2%, etc.).

There are also federal, state and community financing programs that require little or no money down. There is no central clearing house for these types of loans so you will have to do your own homework and check with any local housing authorities for these.

How can you shop for financing when you don't even have a piece of property in mind? You need to tell the lender what you are doing. Let them know that you are looking for a piece of real estate to fix and flip or to rent out. What the lender is interested in is your credit rating. Do you have a good history of paying everything on time? Do you have a good income so that you can afford to make the payments even if you are without a renter for a few months? Do you have a sufficient down payment? Most important, remember that their job is to make as much money off of you as they can.

The down payment needs to come from either money you have saved or some kind of collateral. If you already own the home you live in, have you built up enough equity that you could take a second mortgage on it to cover the down payment? If you are buying rental property, keep in mind that potential rent can be used as part of the income you need to prove you have. Also use any prepaid rents and security deposits to help cover closing costs. We have even heard of younger people borrowing the down payment from friends and family. Personally, we do not suggest this as it is a good way to lose friends and make family get-togethers very difficult.

We feel no one should ever invest money they do not have. Going into even more debt is not going to increase you personal worth or financial value. Of course, if you are determined to risk everything, we cannot stop you. Only you can make the decision to invest relatively safely or to risk everything. If you cannot come up with a sufficient down payment, just wait until you can. Going into even more debt by borrowing the down payment (and/or other fees) is just going to cost you more money and cut into your profit. It can even mean losing money in the end.

The idea for investing in real estate is to use as little of your own money as possible (your down payment) and as much of someone else's money as possible (the lender's money). This is called leverage. If you are simply buying a house to live in and have no desire to invest in any other real estate, then you may want to put down a larger down payment in order to borrow less and have smaller monthly payments. The idea in making money from rentals is to find a place that, when financed, will have a low enough monthly mortgage payment that the rent will cover the payment plus insurance, maintenance and taxes. Sometimes it might even be worth it to have to pay some money out of your own pocket each month for awhile until the property has built up some equity at which point you could refinance it for a smaller monthly payment and/or charge a higher rent price. However, again this is riskier and should only be attempted when you have a sufficient financial cushion and/or you know that in a fairly short time you can increase the rents to now cover your costs..

Let's say you bought a rental property for $200,000 and had a monthly mortgage payment of $1,500. You would need to get rent of at least $1,800 to cover all the expenses. However, you could rent it for $1,400 and pay the rest yourself if you can afford to do so. After three years you could refinance for $180,000 at a monthly rate of $1,200 assuming the interest rates are still the same. Now the rental would cover everything. Also, you may have made improvements or the rental market has improved wherein you can charge a higher rent than 2 years ago. We will discuss this in more detail later.

What most people forget, even when buying their own home, is all the other costs involved in buying and keeping property. For instance, you will be paying for an appraiser, a property inspector, a surveyor, title insurance, and other possible costs. If you are financing more than 80% of the property value, you will also have to pay mortgage insurance for the lender until such time as you have more than 20% equity in the property. This does not include the usual maintenance if you plan on renting the property or the fix-it-up costs for a fix and flip. The easiest way to get an estimate of what these costs will be is by speaking with your real estate agent. And when you do find out the costs, *write them down* in a booklet that you will keep with you and refer to. Do not try to remember everything your real estate broker or banker tells you. And do not rely entirely on what the banker or agent is telling you. You need to do your own research to know what re-roofing a house in your area costs today, how much new good quality appliances are going to cost, etc. Again, remember those things you can do yourself will reduce the costs quoted.

For now though you need to find a lender, how high an amount are they willing to lend you, what is their required down payment, and what other costs are involved. Then you can seriously look at property.

A lot of the get-rich-quick schemes advertised on TV and elsewhere depend on your getting financing from the owner of the property. These situations are very difficult to find and are also very risky and will cost you more. For one thing, you will usually have to pay a higher price to make it worthwhile for the owner to finance it for you. You will also be required to pay a higher interest rate then the prevailing going rate, again to make it worthwhile for the owner. The length of the loan will *usually* be for 10 to 20 years rather than the standard 30 years because the owner wants to get his money, not die while waiting for it. Keep in mind that there has to be a reason why the owner is willing to finance the sale. It might be because they are asking too much so that no realtor could find a buyer at that price. Or it could be that they are looking for a sucker who does not know what is going on so they can sell them property that has some serious problems such as no viable clean water system or restrictions on the use of the property or any number of other things. The seller is hoping to find someone who does not know what they are doing and who does not hire the people necessary to check everything out for them. Deal with a lender who will hold the mortgage on the property and, therefore, will have a vested interest in it.

Remember that any time you pay no money down (on anything) your loan will be for that much more and can easily put you in debt way over your head.

Some people get into lease-with-the-option-to-buy deals. This works well for you, the buyer, if you are sure you can meet all the requirements for down payment, monthly costs, etc. However, keep in mind that statistics show the majority of people who lease with the intention of part of that money going toward the down payment end up leaving and, therefore, forfeiting all that money. Also, your payment will be much higher than it would be with a regular monthly mortgage. The seller makes more and then you leave and they still own the property and wait for the next unsuspecting person to come along.

There are several ways to come up with the necessary down payment. The usual way is to get a second mortgage on your current home using the equity you have built up in it. However, if due to the current economy interest rates have dropped, it might be worthwhile to refinance your current home mortgage also to give you more monthly money you can use on your investment project. Keep in mind that, besides the down payment, you will have additional costs such as closing points that are usually ½% to 1% of the total loan.

We have seen people who have huge yard sales of everything they don't need from old lamps to the boat they haven't used in three years and raised several thousand dollars this way. One family decided they didn't need his rifle collection (as he hadn't been hunting in over 10 years) and she didn't need her silver collection (as she hated cleaning it). After all, interests change over time. What you may have thought was very important to you years ago could now bring in the needed down payment.

We have also seen people make a conscious decision to invest in property and, therefore, each took on a second job with all of that additional income going into an account to save for the purchase of that first property. And, yes, some younger people will actually move back in with the parents in order to save for a new house.

If you do not own any property and must borrow from family and friends, make sure you use an attorney to create a good solid contract so that they and you are protected and to keep peace among friends and family.

Please stay away from the interest only loans and balloon payment loans. These are just asking for trouble. An interest only loan means you will be paying a monthly payment forever and never reducing your loan value as well as not building any equity! A balloon payment means that some day (usually in 5 years) you will have to come up with the total amount due. 99% of our population cannot come up with that balloon payment without taking out another loan. Therefore, you have spent thousands more than you should have with nothing to show for it. And, if you don't qualify for another loan and you can't pay the balloon payment, you may lose the property.

Also, we highly suggest staying away from variable rate loans. These are fine when interest rates are low and expected to stay low. But the reality is that what goes down must eventually go up again. This means, the interest on your mortgage could go up to the point where you cannot afford to pay your mortgage. If you can barely afford your mortgage now, what would happen if you were unemployed? Variable rate loans will usually only help you if you plan on selling or refinancing within 2 years before rates can go up a significant amount.

There are other types of loans that might help you in particular situations. For instance, you might qualify for an FHA loan which will usually also cover the rehab costs on the property. You might qualify for a HUD loan but you must be the occupant of the property for at least one year unless it is not inhabitable at the time of the purchase. If you qualify as a veteran for a VA loan, you will get a very low interest rate and do not have to occupy the building yourself.

But all the financing in the world will not help if you end up paying more than the property is actually worth. You need to find a good deal and that will vary from one type of investment to another.

USING A REAL ESTATE BROKER

After you have found that you can find a good loan with a low interest rate and a low down payment and you know the maximum amount of loan you can afford, you can start looking at property (in that dollar range!). We fully realize that some people simply like looking at property. They have no intention of buying any. Or they think they want to buy but never seem to get around to it usually because they can't make up their minds. If your idea of fun is to spend all your free time researching real estate, then by all means do it. However, we assume you also have other things in your life that you like doing or need to be done. Therefore, finding a *good* real estate agent can save you a lot of time. Actually, we recommend finding 2 or even 3 good ones although you do not want to tell them you are working with another broker as this will make you a "looker" and not a buyer. What is a good real estate agent? Someone who is going to actually work for you. That means actively looking for new properties before they even hit the market. It means letting you know about new listings before they are advertised.

Why 2 or even 3 agents? You need as much help as you can get and if one of them does not seem to be doing anything for you, you will still have a couple of others who will. Make contact with some agents, talk with them, and try to determine if they are go-getters or do they just want the business to come to them. This can take a few weeks to determine because most brokers automatically assume you are just a looker. Unfortunately, most people who make contact with a broker are just looks and the agents know this. So don't be insulted if they do not seem to take you seriously right away. However, if you find yourself doing the searching (online or driving by for sale signs) and pointing out new listings to them, you need to try another agent.

And do not trust anyone! We are not talking about just agents. You cannot trust your lender, contractors or anyone. Sorry we have to sound so negative here but most of you are aware of this. In a business deal you are dealing with people you do not know and you have to be careful at all times. If you decide to extend your real estate holdings over time, you will eventually get to know the people you are working with and learn what you can expect from them. However, for now, check and re-check what anyone tells you. Make sure you follow up on whatever others say they are going to do. We have a good friend who waited till the day before the closing to call the agent to find out where and when it would be only to discover the broker had "forgotten" to take care of scheduling. They had already signed a contract selling their house and allowing the new owners to move in and they were left without any place for themselves to move into!

Even dealing with agents, you will still need to spend time looking for good property (reading the ads, looking at "for sale" signs, going to open houses, checking listings on internet). Besides looking for your own investment, you will need to know what is going on in real estate in your area. However, keep in mind that the ads and such will only tell you about property that is already being offered and after others have already looked at them. If you can find a go-getter agent, tell them what you are looking for (a single family or multi-family unit, an apartment building, a house, a fix and flip unit or a rental property), the price range you are looking for and the locations. Let them do the looking for you. Also, they will quite often learn about new properties coming on the market that you would have to wait to find out about. If it is already on the market and it is a good deal, it will have already been snatched up by someone else. A good agent can save you a lot of time. They will also be familiar with what is going on in general with real estate in your area. However, having said this, we have to admit that we have **never** heard a broker say to us, "Well, property is not moving right now." With brokers, business is always great!

However, they do not save you money as that is not their purpose in life. Their purpose is to make money for themselves. They really are not interested in helping the property seller or buyer unless one of those is going to create income for them. That is, the agent may just want to help the seller move their house quickly and for the price they want so that they will have referrals from a happy customer and receive their commission from a full-price sale. There is nothing wrong with this. That is their business. However, you could also find an agent who knows you will be looking for more property soon and they will want to do everything they can to get your repeat business. In other words, don't worry about the money they make, just remember that a hard working agent can save you a lot of time. Remember that your time is worth a great deal of money so any time they can save you is also saving you dollars.

WHERE TO INVEST

Besides finding out whether you can get financing or not and finding a good real estate agent to help you, you need to decide on where you want to invest.

If you are buying your own home, obviously it will be in the area you will be working in or in an area you wish to commute from. Although your own home is also an investment, when purchasing real estate specifically for the potential profit or income potential, you have a much wider area to consider.

You will find it much safer and easier to invest in your own area rather than traveling to that current hot real estate locale. For one thing, you should understand your local area better than any other area and, the more you understand, the safer your investment will be. It is also easier. We have watched a lot of Californians travel back and forth to Phoenix in order to purchase property during their recent regional inflation. Yes, we go to Phoenix frequently but because we present our seminars there so it was just part of our normal trips. This period or "bubble" of housing inflation was also seen in other cities but not in all cities or in most small towns. We suppose that if you love flying back and forth on an hours notice, you might like investing in some place other than where you live. We certainly love to travel but we live where we do because we like the area and, therefore, wish to spend our spare time here. It is also easier to research and keep track of what is going on in the area you actually live in. However, aside from the difficulty of doing the research and the actual walk through of houses, everything else can be done long distance today using your fax machine, email or over-night delivery. Personally we recommend a very hands-on approach which means you will be doing your own research, you will be doing walk throughs of potential properties, you need to be there when any inspector does his thing, and, if you make a bid, you will be spending a lot of time on the phone (you never know when someone will check their email) and using your fax machine.

You will need to follow the local news carefully. This may be something you already do. If not, subscribe to your local paper. You need to not only read the real estate ads but also know what changes are happening in your area. Do you see prices slowly rising or perhaps quickly rising or are prices dropping? Do you see the same house advertised week after week indicating either a too high price or a slow selling economy? Do you see a large rise in the number of available rental units showing a glut in the market? Are there new large businesses (potential employment producer) coming into the area? Or are large businesses laying off people or even closing down? You must also be alert to changes in construction, zoning, etc. For example, where we live in Sacramento, there is a continuing debate with construction of housing in or near a flood plane. This area is only as good as the levy that holds back the water! Speculators are certainly proceeding to build in these flood plains but personally we are not interested in seeing our property destroyed in a few years. And, yes, we are more ethical. We do not intend to sell someone a house, no matter what our profit would be, that could be doomed from the start.

Living in the area you want to invest in will make you aware of things you need to know. For instance, here in Sacramento we know that housing prices go up every time there is an earthquake along the coast as people want to leave that area and move to a safer area. A lot of people left New Orleans after the hurricane who will never return there as they want a safer location. All areas have their own unsafe things whether they are severe winter storms, flooding, hurricanes, tornadoes, fire danger, or whatever. Some people adjust to these different conditions but some do not and decide to move. Any small or large disaster will cause some people to move creating dropping prices in that area and creating higher prices (as demand increases) in the areas they move to. Keep in mind that, in general, housing prices are higher in the northern part of the country due to winter weather and this keeps prices lower in the southern half where the weather is milder. Northern climates usually have a full foundation and better insulation that adds to the cost while southern houses are usually built on a slab and thus cost less. Added to this is the fact that the costs of running a house or building are usually higher in the northern areas due to higher fuel costs, grocery costs, etc. than in the southern areas of the country.

Local news can also affect prices. A large well-known chain store such as Cabella's moving into an area will create new jobs and bring more people to the area for those jobs creating demand for good housing and rental units. The same thing happens when a sizable business moves into your area. Of course, the opposite will also have an effect. If a large employer lays off a large number of employees or actually closes, people will be leaving the area.

Even if you live in a small town, you know there is an area of rundown homes. Seeing a news report that a group of business people are planning on renovating part of this area could create a good area for you to also invest in. We have actually seen very energetic individuals buy up these run down locations and then create a revitalization of the area by getting the town councils as well as the public's attention. Just as it only takes one run down house in an area to start a whole decline in that neighborhood, restoring just one place can start a whole revitalization in a run down area.

In order to get a good deal, you need to learn what the market values are in the area you want to buy in. One way to get an overview of current values in your area is to go to ofheo.gov (Office of Federal Housing Enterprise Oversight). However, keep in mind that property market values can differ tremendously within one city. One section of your city could be a slum area with great potential if you can afford to fix it up and get others interested in doing the same thing. In this area you will find really good deals. Another section might be a good solid middle class area with a house that needs fixing up. Here you can find a good deal that can be brought up to the market value of the rest of that area. Another section of your city might be a downtown, more commercial area. Again, this could provide a good deal for you. Therefore, you need to research the specific areas of your city that you are interested in investing in to know what the housing values are in that area.

In other words, you need to look at property that is selling for below the current market value (or perhaps at market value) that you can renovate into something profitable. In any case, we suggest starting in the city you live in or a nearby area for convenience. An exception might be a vacation rental unit that could be in another state. Also, after looking at housing for at least 3 weeks, you will get a sense of what housing price values are keeping in mind that these values can and do change as frequently as monthly. After all, this is not the sort of investment you put your money into and then forget about. Real estate investing is an ongoing business even though it is part-time.

What is considered a good deal, however, will vary from one area to another and from one type of property to another. Therefore, finding a good deal will be discussed under each type of property. However, we all like a good deal whether it's buying that $100 dress at half price or buying a house that is currently worth $180,000 but will be made into a $400,000 house.

What you should be looking for is a property that you can buy for what it is valued at or even slightly below that you can change into a higher priced property for a profit. So first you have to decide what kind of property you are looking for – a house to live in, rental unit or units, a fix and flip, a vacation home/rental, or business rental. And the only way to do this is to do the necessary research in your area.

Now that you have figured out the financing, found a broker to work with and you know what area you want to invest in, you need to decide which type of investment is best for you. Do you want to buy a house to fix and flip or to fix and rent out? Do you want to buy a rental unit for income? Do you want to find a vacation home that you can also rent out? Do you want to buy a family home to live in, renovate, and then sell for a good profit? Do you want business property to rent out? This decision will depend a lot on how much time and money you want to put into the property after you have bought it. That is, do you want to do a lot of fixing up with the attendant costs or are you looking for something you can use or rent out immediately without putting any work or money into it? If you are still undecided, the best way to decide which type of investment you want to get into is to look at each type individually.

YOUR OWN HOME

Again, your own home will usually be the biggest investment most families ever make. However, national averages say 7 out of 10 families move at least once and the average homeowner will change homes about 5 times during their lifetime. So, aside from considering what you can afford to buy, you also need to consider resale potential. A lot of couples starting out cannot afford the house of their dreams so they start with a small house with the intention that eventually they will sell it and move to a bigger house as the family grows. This is sometimes referred to as "climbing the property ladder".

It is easier to get financing on this type of property as the bank will know you have good reason to take care of it because you will be living in the house (keep in mind the bank owns your property until the loan is paid off). Owning your own home means you can buy an older house that does need some fixing up but, as it is where you will be living, it also provides you with the time to do renovations at your own pace and as you can afford to do it.

The reason for buying a house may be that you want a home for you and your family. However, we feel you should always be thinking about the future and how to make money from this huge investment. If you are buying your first home on a limited budget, location is very important. You need to be within commuting distance of your work place but this still leaves a huge area to look at. And it is possible even today to find affordable places.

Keep in mind that the value of your home can help you a lot in the future. For instance, let's say you have an emergency come up such as major surgery. You can get a loan using the equity on your home as collateral. This is usually done as a second mortgage.

You will build equity or value in your home in two ways. First is just using time. That is, as years go by, property becomes worth more due to the demand for more homes. Second is the equity you create. This is renovating your home through the years to add value to it. Third is the equity you will build just by slowly paying on your original mortgage amount. Therefore, you can see that even your home is a very good investment. It also beats renting an apartment as you are purchasing a tangible asset instead of collecting a lot or rent receipts.

To buy your home, you need to be constantly looking. Yes, you will have a realtor helping you but they can only do so much. Also, they might be pushing the properties they actually brought in so they will make more commission (without having to split the fee) when that house is sold. Therefore, you need to be looking also. You can easily check the internet for house sales in your area breaking down your search by zip code or city or area plus the numbers of bedrooms you are looking for and the price range you are interested in.

However, if you are looking for a good bargain, there are certain things to watch for. You need to watch for listed properties that have had the asking price reduced.

This could mean that they were simply asking too much to begin with. However, it could also mean they really need to sell this house (in order to move for a new job for instance). When buying a home, do not be afraid to let friends and acquaintances know you are looking. They might know of friends who are going through a divorce and figure the house will have to be sold in the process. They may know of an older person whose spouse died and figure that person will want to move to be near family. As retired bankers, we have known people in that industry who watch for foreclosures because they know the bank is only interested in getting whatever is still owing on the mortgage. Some people we know have become very wealthy using this method. However, you would need this insider information to make this work for you.

Remember that you are looking for a good deal in order to make your home a good investment also. Yes, you could simply buy the home of your dreams and hold onto it until it has appreciated and hope for the best but we are talking about making a profit sooner.

What are you looking for in order to get a good deal?

1. In the photos, do you see an old dark kitchen that you could freshen up with pale yellow walls and paint the cabinets white? Do the cabinets look like they need replacing? Does the front of the house need full landscaping to make it more appealing or is it simply overgrown and needs a little work?

2. Considering the apparent condition of the property (by the photos) and its location, is the house

priced at market value? Market value means what is the average cost for a home in the same area in the same condition. If it is priced over the market value, are you interested enough to make a low bid and see if it is accepted? If it is priced below market value, you will need to look at it in person to determine why it is.

3. Is it in a good location? You have heard over and over again that location is everything. However, you will not be able to determine a lot about the location until you actually look at the house.

Get together a list of several places you want to look at plus whatever the realtor has found for you and have the realtor make appointments for you to see these places. Unfortunately, the best time to see them is during the week. Obviously at night you will not be able to see everything in the dark. Weekends cause problems in that the owners need to be out of the house plus this is the busiest time for realtors. You may need to take some time off from work but, if that is not possible, do your looking on weekends.

Make sure you dress comfortably for your shopping expedition. Bring along a note pad and pen as you will need to make a lot of notes or go to an office supply store to get a general purpose appraisal form for houses to save time and to make sure you don't forget anything important. You will also find an inexpensive digital camera useful to record certain features you like or that need improving.

1. As you drive up to the house, look at the neighborhood. Are all of the other houses in excellent condition? If yours is not, then you have potential for a

good buy as all you have to do is bring it back up to par with the neighborhood. Or are the other homes mixed as in some in excellent condition, some are okay, or maybe a few need better upkeep? This can mean several different things. If you see a mixed bag, it could mean the neighborhood is slowly going down hill. However, this mixed condition neighborhood could also mean that it is on the way up and some people are already fixing up their own homes. The only way to determine this is to research which of those homes have been recently bought and for how much. If you see a lot of property changing hands recently, has the market value of those homes gone up or down or stayed the same since they were purchased? If they were obviously bought below market value and now seem to be well taken care of, you are looking at an area that is going up in value. Also look to see if there are children and other people on the street or is it quiet. Is there graffiti on walls or signs or indications that graffiti has been painted over? If so than this neighborhood could have gang problems. Ideally, you should be looking at a house that is in a neighborhood of good middle-class to upper-class homes that just needs a little work to get the best buy. However, you could also see that the outside of the house looks fine and fits in with the rest of the area's homes just fine. Also, note if you see any other houses for sale or for rent signs as this could mean people are leaving this neighborhood for a reason. It is your job to find out what those reasons are.

Are prices high right now and people are taking their profit in the higher equity to buy a new home? This means prices are high. However, you could be looking at the same neighborhood right after a "bubble" has burst where people have already bought new homes and now can't sell the old one for what they thought they were going to get. Now their only choice is to try to rent it out till prices go back up again. This is where your research should tell you or at least give you a good indication of what is going on.

Now you need to take a look inside. Remember to write down notes on everything you are seeing and take photos!

2. You need to look at each individual room in the house and keep good notes of what you are seeing. If possible, bring along that digital camera so you can actually take pictures of the problem areas as well as the good areas. Keep in mind that problems are only problems if they are too costly or difficult to fix. If you see things that you know you can fix yourself at a reasonable cost or that would be worth hiring someone to fix for you, then these are not problems. Part of your ongoing research is to visit Home Depot and Lowe's a great deal to know what materials are costing today so you will have an idea as to how costly these repairs might be. Again, keeping detailed notes is very important. What do you need to check?

Kitchen – Look at the condition of the flooring, the walls, the cabinets, the appliances, and the lighting. Look inside all cupboards and under the sink. Are there any signs of leaking water as in water stains? Does the flooring need replacing and updating? Do the cupboards need replacing or would a coat of paint do wonders for their appearance? Are the appliances in good condition or do some need replacing? Are the appliances being sold with the house or will you need to buy new ones? Is the lighting up to date or does it need updating? Does the faucet have a good strong flow of water? Is there plenty of natural lighting or does the kitchen seem dark? If so, is there a place to add new windows to bring in more natural light or will new lighting have to suffice?

Living/Family rooms – Check the condition of the flooring. Does it need new carpeting or simply a good cleaning? In some areas of the country tile flooring is preferred over carpeting so you might need to think about replacing the flooring. Do the walls need painting or are they white and need color added to make the room more appealing? Is the ceiling in good condition or does it show signs of repairs or water staining? Does it have sufficient electrical outlets? Does it need more lighting to brighten the place up?

Bedrooms – How many bedrooms are there? A three or four bedroom house is worth a lot more than a two bedroom house which is worth more than a one bedroom house. Again, is the floor covering in good condition or does it need replacing? Are the walls and ceiling in good condition or are there signs of previous damage or water stains? Would fresh paint add to the value of the house? Check for closet size. Is there sufficient storage room? Or will the closet size detract from the house? Is there a master bedroom and, if so, how large or small is it? Is there a bathroom attached to the master bedroom?

Bathrooms – How many bathrooms are there? Unless it is a very small house (one or two bedroom), you should have at least two bathrooms. If the house is two stories, it should have at least one bathroom on each floor for maximum sale price. If it does not, can you add a bathroom? Check out the flooring, the cabinets, the condition of the toilet (flush it!) and sink and tub/shower (turn it on!), and look for any signs of damage or water stains. Does it have tile on the floor and in the shower or is it just linoleum and a fiberglass enclosure that you could change to tile to increase the value?

3. There are other miscellaneous things to watch for such as are there sufficient electrical outlets of sufficient size for today's demanding electrical use, is the plumbing made of PVC piping or is it an old house that might need to have the plumbing replaced? Is there a laundry area in a convenient location? Will the appliances be selling with the house or not? Are there any other things such as drapes or fixtures that will stay with the house? Or are there things you would like to stay with the house that you might be able to negotiate for?

4. Outdoors – Walk around the back and side yards checking for the quality of the grass (does it need replacing) or landscaping. Note any trees, shrubs, or perennial plantings and how much work would be needed to fix up the yard. Is there storage area either in a shed building or in a side yard out of sight? Is there a patio/deck in good condition or does it need repair? If there is no deck/patio, is there room to add one, preferably with a pergola or awning over it?

Check the front yard not only to see if it is in acceptable condition but does it appeal to you. That is, is the front just plain boring? Could it be fixed up to look better from the street? Would painting or replacing the walkway or the front door improve the appeal from the entrance? Does the entire exterior need painting? Carefully check the condition of the siding for possible damage or repairs. Step back and look at the roof for any missing shingles or obviously repaired areas. Does it need to be re-roofed? Also check for dry rot and insect damage to the house, as best you can (you will need an inspector for this also if you decide to bid on it) especially in southern climates where termite damage can be expensive. How is it heated and cooled and are these units in good condition or are they antiquated and not energy efficient?

Is there a garage and is it for one or two cars? Does it have a garage door opener and what condition are the garage doors in? Are the driveway and any walkways in good condition?

Stand quietly and look around the neighborhood. How is the noise level (and what time of day is it)? If it is quiet in the middle of the day and you think you want to put in a bid on this house, come back that evening to check out the night scene for noise or any gang activity. It is particularly good to check on a Friday or Saturday night as that is when things will be the worst. Does the neighborhood look appealing or run down or even threatening?

5. If you decide to put in a bid on this house, make sure it is contingent on getting all the necessary inspections done before the closing. That is, you are not a plumber so get a plumber in to check any possible problem areas. If you think the roof might need replacing, get an actual estimate. Whether your state requires one or not, hire a building inspector and go over the entire property with him. This is money well spent and usually runs anywhere from $150 to $300. Finding out about major problems after you have purchased a house is too late and very expensive!

By the end of the day you should have a lot of notes and pictures to check over. For each house you will need to compare the asking price with the actual market value of houses for that neighborhood. Then you need to estimate the cost involved in any repairs or remodeling that you think is necessary. For now, you can just estimate this yourself if you are familiar with the going rates. How much of your time will be involved in painting and fixing to make this house more comfortable? Keep in mind that not every little thing has to be perfect and how much work you do on the house will depend on how you like to live.

If you are looking for a home to live in that will appreciate in value, then you will be willing to pay the market value of the house. By living in it you will have all the time you need to fix or change things and you will have the time growth of the equity in the house. It also means you will be able to spread out the cost involved in the fixing and changing over a longer period of time. So even if you pay the market value of the house, it should appreciate over time from the fixing and changes you do as well as the natural increase over time of the value of housing. The biggest foreseeable problem is whether the prices of homes in that area will stagnate because the neighborhood is going down hill or if prices will increase with time plus the work you put into the house and no one has a crystal ball to know for sure what will happen.

Of course, time will vary for each of you. You may be looking for a place to live in for a year and then you plan on selling it for a profit to finance a bigger home. In this case, you will need to be able to afford to make those changes within just one year as that is the only appreciation you will see. Unless you happen to be in the middle of a strange real estate "bubble", you will generally need more than one year for the house to naturally appreciate in value. In fact, there could be an economic recession that devalues your house and you will need to change your plans in order to wait until the recession is over to sell that house.

To decide on whether to make an offer on this particular house, you need to follow the following formula in order to get a good deal:

Asking price + loan costs + cost of repairs = Market value (or less)

Keep in mind that you need to know all of the loan costs involved including the monthly mortgage payment plus taxes and insurance and upkeep costs. If you cannot afford that payment **and** the costs involved, then you cannot afford this house. Do not depend on the lending institutions to answer your questions about what other costs are involved. Also ask your realtor what costs could be involved as they will be very familiar with what different lenders require but may not be telling you.

However, if you plan on living in this house for several years, the formula is slightly different in that you do not have to include the cost of repairs and remodeling as this will be done over a longer period of time as the house is appreciating anyway.

Be sure to check for any neighborhood covenants or associations that might restrict you in improving or change your property. For instance, you might not be allowed to change the siding to stucco when everyone else has clapboard siding.

Finally, you need to be aware of any unusual circumstances that might force the seller into a lower price. For instance, is the house being sold due to a divorce or impending bankruptcy or a job move? These all give you more negotiating leverage. If you own an RV or boat, is there room to store it on the property and is this allowed?

Making The Deal

Once you have found the property you want you need to make an offer. It is one thing to offer less then what the market value is, it is another thing to be reasonable. That is, this is not a science. No one can give you some percentage that you should subtract from the asking price to offer the seller. There are other things that influence how good a deal you can make.

If houses in your area are selling in a matter of days, then there will be little room for negotiation. You can track property that you find online as to how long they stay on the market or go to your real estate agent and they can provide a list of comparable properties and how long they were on the market. Perhaps you run into a situation where a housing "bubble" has caused a lot of owners to buy new and bigger homes using the unexpected appreciation from the sale of their former home as down payment. If the "bubble" is still going on, they will probably be able to sell for the asking price and in a short amount of time (sometimes within 24 hours). However, we have seen what happens with the downside of the "bubble" when prices are beginning to fall. That is, the home owner has already bought the new home only to find that their old home is no longer worth what it was just a few weeks ago. Now they have to sell at a lower price in order to get rid of it or they attempt to rent it out hoping the prices will go back up. It is not unusual in this situation to see a lot of former family homes with "for rent" signs in front of them. We have seen two and three houses in a row on one street trying to rent. If they are asking too much rental (in order to pay the first monthly mortgage payment) you can probably pick these places up for less then the market value. If you have the time, you can wait until the renters have caused wear and tear on the place, and then make an offer.

To negotiate a good price, you need to do several things. First, check out the history of that house through municipal records to see how often this property has changed hands and if there are any liens on it. Check online or with your broker to see how long the property has been on the market and if there have been any price reductions indicating the owners are getting anxious to sell. Check with the town's planning board for any possible rezoning, variances, new roads or new construction that will be occurring in the area that could devalue the house or add to the value. Now find out what the market value is based on what other similar properties are currently selling for. Then you bid below that and make sure you do not pay more then the market value.

Your first offer should be substantially below the asking price but do not be unreasonable. You need to have it low enough to give you some negotiating room. However, if houses are selling quickly, you will not have any bargaining power anyway so you need to decide whether you want to live in this home or not. Obviously, when prices are high is *not* the time to be buying property. It might be better for you financially to rent a place for awhile and keep watching and waiting for the prices to start going down or, for the best deal, wait until prices have dropped as far as you think they will.

Negotiating is getting some of what you want and giving up some things also. After all of this research, it is very important that you write down the lowest bid you feel you can make on this property *and* how high you are willing to go in the negotiations. Keep this note posted where you can always see it so you do not get carried away and end up offering more than you know you should. The worst thing you can do is fall in love with a house and thus end up paying more than you should for it. That higher mortgage payment may be fine right now with your new job, but how will you pay it when your company cuts back and you are looking for another job? Only buy what you can afford!

You will make the first offer. You will usually be required to give earnest money ($500 to $2,000) that will be put in escrow to show that you are serious about this purchase. If this is rejected, you can now increase your offer and/or add things you want the owner to do or provide. Perhaps you are willing to go a little higher if they will include the appliances with the sale. Check your list you made of everything inside and outside to show them that there is a lot of work to be done so they can decide whether to do the work themselves and charge more or charge less and let you do the work. Perhaps you can negotiate wherein the seller will pay some or all of the closing costs, the inspection costs, title insurance, mortgage points, transfer taxes, or any tests that need to be done. Always keep the market value in mind and never go over that unless you are certain this property is going to become worth more then it is today or you plan on living in it for a long time.

Make sure the realtor is using a standard contract. If you are dealing directly with the owner without an agent involved, hire an attorney and he can provide you with a standard contract. Keep in mind that it is very difficult (contrary to what those seminars tell you) to get a good deal directly through the owner. They could be selling without an agent because they are asking so much that no agent can sell it for them. Or they could be trying to pull something on you assuming that, without an agent to guide you, you don't know what you are doing and he can get away with selling you the well that has not passed water tests in 10 years or the rotten support beams. Most states usually have a disclosure law whereby the seller is supposed to state know problems or defects such as there is lead-based paint in the house. However, this is not fool proof as the owner may not know, or claims de does not know, of any such problems.

We fully realize that probably 99% of all Americans do not read any contract they sign. However, we feel we must fight these odds and tell you to please read the contract. If you do not understand something in it, ask for an explanation and keep asking until you understand everything. Never accept a verbal promise such as, "We will take care of that" or "That's already covered in the contract." If it is in the contract, have them show you where. And do not take any verbal promises. Always get it in writing! We hope that you are operating honestly but that does not mean the other person is.

Always remember that this is a business deal and you need to act appropriately. That is, always be pleasant and smile. Even if you plan on making the house your home, it is still a business deal. It is more professional to pleasantly back away from a deal that will not benefit you instead of making demands and threats. Try to reason with the seller. Perhaps you could point out how long the house has already been on the market and that there are more and more rentals in the neighborhood which will force their asking price down. Perhaps a few months later when they see more houses on their street with un-mown lawns and broken windows and a junk car on the street, they will be willing to lower the sale price. Always keep your options open. After all, you know there are lots of other houses out there.

Selling For A Profit

However, assuming you are planning on reselling fairly soon for the profit, you need to decide which projects are important and which ones will not really help with the appreciation potential. The following are the most cost effective.

1. Clean everything thoroughly. This doesn't cost you enough to say so other than your time and effort but makes a huge difference when trying to sell property.

2. Add spice to the house with color. Painting (both inside and out) is a relatively inexpensive way to add value to a house and it is something you can learn to do quite well yourself. It is said that you will get 10 times what the paint cost you in return. Color can add that warmth that people want to see in their potential family

home. Neutral earth tones are the best way to get that color and warmth.

3. Add extras that buyers would appreciate such as tile or wood floors (depending on what area of country you live in). Today you can even do either of these things yourself. Granite countertops are very popular right now. Personally, we would never have granite as it stains so easily but they do command a higher price right now.

4. Today people want lots of room so that it can actually be cost effective to add a second floor or put an addition on a house. This is especially true if you are adding bedrooms and/or bathrooms. However, be sure to see if you can even get a permit for this or not before you bid on the house. Particularly with newer homes, the lots are so small there is no room to add anything. Keep this in mind when looking for a good deal. If it is just the two of you, a small home is fine. But, as the family grows, is there the possibility of adding onto the house rather than having to move again?

5. Create a good view. Your house may look out on an alley way but that does not mean it has to look depressing. You could add a new fence or paint the old one. Add some plants or simply hang window boxes with tall plantings so people will see the flowers and not the alley. People do not want to see just lawn in a back yard or just desert. However, neither do they want to do a lot of work on it. So can you add shrubbery and perennial flowering plants that need care only every two to four years? Mother Nature can just about always improve any view.

6. People want their homes to have plenty of light. This may mean adding more lighting to a room or actually changing out the windows (insulated windows bring a higher price).

7. People want quiet peaceful homes so, before buying, check out the neighborhood morning, noon and night for partying, boom boxes going by, etc.

8. Make any necessary repairs rather than trying to sell something that is broken. A broken window might cost you $200 to replace and not add any value to the house. But *not* replacing that broken window can take $200 off your asking price very quickly. It will also give the perception to a prospective buyer that other things might need fixing or replacing.

Most of these things can be done relatively inexpensively. However, the more you add to a home, the more it will be worth (usually). But you don't want to make the mistake of fixing something or adding something that will not add to the value. So what are buyers looking for?

1. New updated kitchens (new cabinets and appliances, preferably stainless steel) with lots of windows for light add from 20% to 50% onto the value of your property depending on what area of the country you are in.

2. Updating a bathroom with tile and new fixtures or adding a bathroom add another 20% or even more if you are starting with just one bathroom. Ideally there should be at least one bathroom for each floor.

3. If you are in warm climates, create outdoor space as in a covered patio or deck. This will add another 20% to 30%. However, even in areas with snow people want a deck to enjoy the summer weather. Keep in mind that there should be some sort of covering for the deck such as a pergola or awning.

4. If you are in colder climates, increasing the insulation value in the walls and attic can add another 10% to the value.

5. Painting the entire house, inside and out, and replacing any worn flooring will increase the value.

6. Adding a garage (should have at least a one-car garage but room for two or more will add even more value) will add value to the house.

7. Putting on a new roof will add value especially if it has a 30 year or longer warranty.

8. Can you add closet space or, better yet, a walk-in closet for storage? Depending on the house, this may or may not be possible but any extra storage space adds value.

9. Landscaping does not add a great deal of value (unless the building is surrounded by a weed patch) but does shorten the time it takes to sell the property because people will immediately see landscaping that puts a smile on their face. First impressions really do count so make sure the front entry side is neat and attractive.

These are all things that will cost you money but will add value to the property. Keep in mind there are also things that cost you a great deal and you will usually not be able to get your money back on it. For instance, doing anything to improve the internal structure or foundation, getting rid of water seepage problems, decontaminating soil, removing lead paint, getting rid of termites and repairing the damage, drilling a new well, creating a new septic system, or chimney repairs will all cost a great deal and can be required by law but usually will not create profit for you.

When buying your first home, you should realize up front that there will be repairs to be made and projects to accomplish. If you really are not into even touching a hammer or screw driver, you will need to hire someone to do all of this for you. However, even if you are not handy, a lot of these things you can do yourself. You can also learn some of these trades free of charge by going over to your local Home Depot or Lowe's and attending their "how to do it" seminars. After all, these are things you will need to do at one time or another as a home owner. The more you can do, the bigger your profit will be when you sell. However, this brings us to one of the biggest mistakes we see people make. You must get proper quotes for the work to be done. If you are doing the work, then go to Home Depot or Lowe's and, using your list of things the house needs, write down what everything costs down to the last penny. Some work you cannot and should not do yourself such as electrical work or plumbing. Anything a contractor will be doing you should get at least 3 bids on. Before accepting a bid, you need to check out each contractor's references and previous work done, their licenses, their insurance coverage, and whether the attorney general's office has any complaints against them.

Too often people guess at what something is going to cost only to find out they were way off. Get those bids and then add on another 20% for the things you forgot about! Also, if you hire a contractor, do not **ADD** anything to the original bid once work has started as this will cost you plenty! If you didn't think of it originally, then it probably wasn't that important anyway. If you feel you absolutely must add this new change, get another bid for it and even see if you can do it yourself. Contractors live for those who decide to add a little extra to the work.

We want to mention something we have previously discussed. That is, when you want to sell your property, you could lease it with the option to buy. As we said previously, this is not the best plan when you want to buy a house. However, it might work for you when you want to sell it. If you must sell during an economic recession or when prices are low, you could make a deal to lease your house with 50% of each months payment going toward the eventual down payment (make sure you have a lawyer work with you on this type of contract). With this you can charge much more than a normal monthly rental would be, usually these types of buyers will take better care of "their" property, while less than 50% of these leases actually end up buying your property so you have a bigger profit. However, having done this before, it is not something we would recommend under normal circumstances but could be used in an emergency sale situation.

Always use a broker to sell the property. We have had many friends who decided to sell their homes themselves in order to save the broker's commission of 3% to 10%. What they learned is that you usually save nothing because you will be spending your money to advertise the house and you will use your own time to show the house (your time is worth money). Also, the broker will do a credit check first thing in order to discourage any lookers and those that will not qualify for a mortgage. Besides the agent's commission is tax deductible.

One other aspect you want to keep in mind when selling a house. When you decide to move to a new location, rather than sell the old house, you might want to keep it as a rental unit to bring in extra income. Keep in mind that there are families moving into areas for job reasons that do not have the down payment for a house and are looking to rent. Also, young people fresh out of school with their first job will usually rent instead of buying a house. And do not rule out students. We have a family house that we rent to a student who was tired of living in cheap rundown apartments. She is responsible for renting out the other two bedrooms. In fact, she actually charges enough that she pays virtually nothing. This also works well for people looking for some extra income. If your kids are already grown and gone and you find yourself with a spare bedroom or two, you could rent those out to college students (with kitchen privileges) for another $500 to $1,000 additional income each month.

*****

Foreclosure Property

One of the types of property the get rich quick schemes talk about is buying foreclosed property. This might be something you are interested in if you have a lot more time to put into this.

First, you could find someone trying to sell their house before foreclosure proceedings start. However, usually the owner owes more than the house is actually worth or they file bankruptcy before foreclosure in order to save their home. Your real estate agent will know if there are any situations like this. However, once the lender has foreclosed, you will have to deal with that lender. When they foreclose, they buy back the property usually for $1 more than is owed on it. Thus they want to sell if for what was remaining on the mortgage plus that $1 and they want to sell quickly. However, be aware that these are usually cash sales as in you have to pay the entire amount in cash that day. In fact, they usually will not even allow time for any inspections. Usually not a good deal and very tricky.

You can also find foreclosed properties at HUD.gov. Keep in mind that you must be going to occupy this residence unless it is a fixer-upper. You are responsible for all inspections before you even make a bid. Thus, if you do not win that bid, you could be out $300 or so just for the inspections.

There are numerous seminars on purchasing foreclosed property or property with tax liens. While this is possible, usually the red tape, timing, etc. is so much that it really requires a tremendous amount of time and stamina. Also, usually by the time it goes to foreclosure, the choicest pieces of property have already been resold.

Once you have your own home to live in, you may decide that investing in real estate is the thing for you. Keep in mind that the above listing of things to look for and what to do when you want to sell property will be used in the following investment properties also.

FIX AND FLIP HOUSE

This is an intriguing method of investment for so many people because it claims to promise quick rewards. The idea is to buy a house, fix it quickly, and then sell it for a huge profit.

First you need to determine what kind of financing you can get and for how much. Then you need to decide on the location. Because you will usually not be living in this house and assuming you have a regular job you have to go to each day, it is best to stick to your own area of the country. This gives you time to work on this house evenings and weekends and to drop in and make sure the contractor you hired is doing what he is supposed to do.

However, the condition of the house is what will give you the profit. You need to find a place in need of renovating in order to buy it for a low price but that you can afford to fix fairly quickly and for a large profit.

Again, look for places that have been reducing their asking price or for a place that is in a mixed neighborhood. Keep in mind that the mixed neighborhood may be on the way down but you could also be its savior. Or that totally rundown area could be brought back by you and you could make money doing it. Certainly when you are starting out on a fix and flip career you want to start small as in doing just one building to see whether you even like the process or did it drive you over the edge! However, if you have

58

tried it and liked it, you can expand by buying into a rundown area, fixing and flipping that first house, in order to use the profit to fix and flip another house in that neighborhood. But make sure this is what you really want to do before getting involved in a totally rundown area. For now, concentrate on a fixed area looking for that one house that needs work.

You will need to put in the research time to check out what market values are for different areas. It is particularly important now that you find a really low priced house that can be rejuvenated. Again, have your realtor set appointments for you to look at the places you have found and that they may know of also. Bring along that paper and pen and the digital camera. However, this is not the only way to find a good buy.

Again, look for the places that must be sold because of divorce, people having to move to a new job location, and those places that are for rent right now but the owners want to sell them.

Be sure to check all the things previously mentioned when looking at a property. Does this place need painting and a little landscaping to give it more value? Besides the usual cleaning and painting, are there other renovations that would quickly increase the value. Most important is to calculate how long it will take you to make these changes and exactly how much it will cost you (get quotes from contractors if necessary).

Does the house need painting and landscaping? Can you create a pleasing garden area that people will immediately want? Is there a space for an outdoor patio or deck? These are all relatively inexpensive things that you can do yourself in a short amount of time.

The inside renovations will usually cost more but have the potential for huge profits. Some of the biggest problems to watch for are:

1. Is the house big enough considering that people today do want lots of room. If not, is it possible to create more room. This could involve adding on a room or creating a whole new second floor. However, putting on a second floor will be very time consuming and quite expensive.

2. One of the biggest costs that will bring one of the biggest profits is modernizing the kitchen. We are not talking about just painting cupboards. How much will it cost you to put in all new cupboards (solid wood of decent quality), new appliances (preferably stainless steel), new countertops (preferably granite), new flooring (tile or stone), and even create more light by installing more lighting or even adding more windows or bigger windows then what is already there.

3. The next biggest profit maker are the bathrooms. People want a master bedroom with its own master bath. Is there such a place or can one be created? If there is no room to add any baths (keeping in mind that you need a minimum of two), you will need to renovate what is there. How much will it cost you for tearing out the old fiberglass tub or shower and putting in a tile surround? Is the toilet in good condition or does that need repairing or even replacing? How much for a new vanity and sink? Or, if it is a small cramped bathroom, what can you do to make it

look bigger such as putting in a free standing sink with lots of mirrors and shelving? Again, the flooring should be tile.

4. Particularly in warmer climates, creating an outdoor room will give the feeling of more actual living room. How much will that deck or patio cost with the pergola or awning and the necessary landscaping?

5. If the house is older, replacing the old windows with new super insulated ones will bring a higher price so long as you remember to actually use that as a selling point.

6. Although these changes will bring you the highest profit, it does not mean you can neglect the rest of the house. Fresh paint in all rooms is a necessity. Flooring needs to be in excellent condition in order to get top dollar. People want lots of light either through extra lighting or more or bigger widows.

7. Always keep in mind that most people do not have good imaginations. Therefore, you will need some furniture so that potential buyers can see how the house will actually look when they move in. Fortunately, the minimal look is very in today so all you need is the basic furniture. Keep in mind that you don't have to buy this furniture either as you can rent it month by month.

8. When it comes time to sell the house, keep in mind that a fresh baked pie on the counter adds a great smell to any house and a flower arrangement or two will create immediate smiles.

However, some things will not add to the value such as pools and saunas or adding a garage in southern climates.

As you look at potential property, list all the things that are good and bad (need fixing or replacing) and take pictures. Then get your estimates. Again, whatever you can do yourself is money in your pocket. If you do need to contract out some work, get at least three bids.

Finally, and most importantly, how fast can you get this work done. If you are dealing with a contractor, get in writing how long the project will take keeping in mind that you will still need to follow up with them every single day they are on the job to make sure things are getting done. Calculate how long it will take for you to do the things you can yourself.

Let's say you get a good deal on a house for $200,000 of which you had to provide a $40,000 down payment. Your monthly mortgage payment is about $1200. You have to spend $30,000 on renovations. Now let's say that it takes you two months to complete all the renovations and then it takes two more months to find a buyer and actually complete the sale. This means you have spent $84,800 out of your pocket. You will need to sell the house for at least $274,800 in order to break even. However, if the renovations and the current economy work in your favor, perhaps you can now sell the property for $300,000 making a $25,200 profit (less the broker's commission fee). This is not to say that you could not make even more. You might be able to create enough value to sell the house for $400,000. However, personally we feel you should always over estimate on what your costs and time will be and underestimate what the selling price will be. It is much better to have made some profit than to have miscalculated and lose money on the deal.

A good friend of ours, let's call her Sally, did everything we just mentioned but happened to finish up as a financial recession was just beginning in her area due to two large businesses closing. It took her almost a year to sell the house and it only sold then because she had dropped the price enough to find a retired couple to buy it. Her $200,000 house with $40,000 worth of renovations ended up costing her over $290,000 and she was only able to get $285,000 for the house. However, she had become too discouraged and simply wanted to get out of the whole situation. Otherwise she could have tried renting it out for awhile to cover the mortgage and costs and wait for the prices to go back up. Or she could have leased it out with the option to buy. If the lease buyers actually carried through and bought the house, Sally would have made a very large profit from the house. And if they left without buying, she still would have made excellent money and then offered it to another buyer. What we are saying is, keep your options open and think about the risks involved before you get into this type of investment.

As mentioned earlier, this could be the start of a new fix and flip business for you if you find you thrive on the mayhem, confusion, frustrations, the feeling of accomplishment and the profit you make.

We make our home in California because this is the weather we enjoy, this is where our children and friends are, and where we have established our gardens and orchard. This is where we want to live. However, we also have rental property that we can use to buy more property with but will also give us a good income when we do not want to expand our real estate investments any more.

APARTMENT RENTAL INCOME

We are partial to rental property for some very good reasons. First, we like doing the work ourselves for the feeling of accomplishment it gives us and rentals allow us to take more time to do it. However, we also like the fact that the rental income will be paying for the mortgage payments, the taxes, the usual maintenance, and the renovations so we do not have to take any money for these things out of our own pocket. We also like the fact that the property is appreciating in value giving us an extra cushion in case of an emergency such as large medical costs. We particularly like the fact that as any changes and renovations are made we will be able to keep increasing the rent we charge. We may start out with the rent just covering the costs but know that over time we will have additional income on top of these costs plus be able to sell it, if necessary or when we want to truly retire, for a good profit.

However, we are hands-on kind of people. You may not be. You may not want to contend with renters or having to redo everything when that renter leaves. Or maybe you really do not want to have to evict anyone. If you cannot handle these types of things, you can hire a rental management agency to do this for you. However, from experience we have to say that you still have to follow up with these people continually to make sure they are doing their jobs. If you want the advantages of rental property but not the headaches, remember that the fee to the agent is also tax deductible.

However, there are different kinds of rental property. For this section we are referring to a rental unit that could be a duplex (2 rental units), a triplex (3 rental units) or a quadplex (4 units). As we have already mentioned, a single family home can also be used as rental property for a family or for several young people living together and sharing the rent. Always remember that you can charge more for a 3 bedroom place then you can for a 1 or 2 bedroom unit. However, if you are concerned about the damage children can do, you might prefer to look at 1 or 2 bedroom places. You could look for a small apartment building keeping in mind that it will involve a lot more money, time and fixing up. We will talk about commercial rental later.

Buying rental property also works for someone who is just starting out and does not own their own home yet in that they can buy a rental unit such as a duplex (instead of a house) and live in one of the apartments while renting out the other one. This gives you a place to live that you can work on fixing up while you are there. You also usually get better interest rates on such a mortgage if you will actually be living on the premises. Also, the other rental unit provides income to help with your monthly morgage payment, taxes, etc. However, everything we talked about in the previous chapter on buying, creating equity in, and selling your own home also applies to rental property.

The first thing to consider is where you want to buy property. You can certainly buy in another state but do you want to do the traveling back and forth for the purchasing process as well as to keep an eye on things? Buying in a distant location usually requires hiring someone to handle collection of rental, maintenance, etc. Therefore, we usually recommend again that you stay in your own area that you already know and understand. Having said this, we admit we have had units in other cities but we are also used to traveling a great deal so we know we will be in those cities two or three times a year anyway. But even we have to admit that managing property where you actually live is much easier.

First you will need to see if you are eligible for the required financing. Then you need to do the research in your area to see what the market value is for these types of properties. You should pretend to be looking for an apartment yourself to see what you get and for how much rental in different areas. Checking out the competition will show you how to out sell them as in what can you provide that they don't and thus charge more for. You will also want to let two or three real estate agents know what you are looking for. However, judging the market price of a rental unit can vary slightly from judging the value of your own home.

When deciding whether to buy this unit or not, there are several factors you need to calculate.

1. What is the going rate in that area for an equivalent rental unit? And are there any indications that this rate will be going up or down in the near future? Or do you see renovations you can do that will cause people to be willing to pay a higher rental amount?

2. For this particular unit, what should the normal maintenance costs be? Be sure to see the previous owner's tax returns and financial books for the previous two years to see how much they were claiming for maintenance. Do the numbers! Make sure there are no "mistakes" in the financials. You need to make the final closing contingent on getting this information, having time to look it over, and finding it satisfactory. If it is not what you expected or wanted, you would then have the right to cancel the contract. This is also a reasonable request as this is considered a business and you have to make a business decision.

3. What have the taxes been on this property over the past five years? Have they been staying the same or going up? Do they seem too high and you think you might be able to get the tax assessor to reduce the taxes (most property taxes are set too high for the local going rate nationwide).

4. What is the market value of this property (not the asking price)?

5. How would tax benefits from owning this unit help your tax situation (see below)?

Ideally, the rent charged should cover the monthly mortgage payment plus the maintenance costs plus the taxes on this property. We assume the renters will be paying their own utilities costs. You should either make a profit from day one or know that in a year you will be making some profit from the rental due to improvements, lowered taxes, increasing cost of living, etc.

However, the question is, should it just cover these things or should there be excess left over for you? This will depend on your personal situation.

For instance, let's say the market value of the triplex is $300,000 giving you a mortgage payment of about $2850 a month (depending on interest rate and length of loan). If you are allowing $100 a month for normal maintenance and $200 a month toward the annual property taxes and insurance, you would have to rent each of the three units for about $1050 a month to cover everything. Is this what units in your area are already getting? If not, there are two things to consider. Either it is not a good deal for you or can you do things to the property that would make it more appealing and thus worth it to people to pay a higher rent then the going rate?

For instance, perhaps all of the units need new carpeting, new appliances, and overall painting and general maintenance. You will need to calculate exactly how much it will cost for all this keeping in mind that you could set up a plan for doing just so much renovation each year. Do you see other units that have been thus renovated renting for higher amounts? If so, it might be worth it to you to buy this property knowing you will just be barely covering expenses but knowing that each year you will be updating one unit and, therefore, increasing that unit's rent. A friend of ours did this with a duplex. They lived in the upstairs unit while renting out the downstairs unit. During the course of a year they completely renovated the upstairs unit they were in with new appliances, painting, and carpeting. They had made a pre-rental agreement with the other tenant that after 12 months, they would switch units but their rental on the new updated one would be more. The tenant decided to look for another place rather than pay the higher rent. Because this was decided the year before when the renter was required to sign the next years lease, this gave the owners a year to find another renter for the new updated upstairs unit. The owners simply moved to the downstairs unit and were still able to find a tenant willing to pay that higher rent for a much nicer unit. They then did the same renovating with the downstairs, bought another duplex, and rented out that downstairs unit. Within two years the two units were renting for $125 more a month then their monthly costs. Obviously you could do this in a shorter amount of time or take even longer to do the renovations. But this does give you the option of deciding how long you want to take and how you want to space the costs out.

You might also want to keep in mind that, if you invest in a 3 or 4 unit building (triplex or quadplex), you will have more units to rent out while working on one of them and you are more likely to have 3 out of 4 units rented at any one time with just one unit left that you need to find a renter for.

We have also known people to buy rental units knowing that the monthly rental income would not cover all of the monthly expenses but knowing that the renovations would quickly make the property worth more rental income. They gambled that spending an extra $100 or so out of their own pocket each month would be quickly recovered upon completion of the renovations. However, our own choice is to at least break even right from the beginning.

You could also be looking at another property that is in very good condition and is, therefore, getting as much rent as possible. Is it worth it to you to buy at the current market value considering that the rental charged should increase every two or three years? At the same time, as more of the mortgage is paid off, you will have more equity in the property that you can use to expand into another rental unit.

Let's say you find a property that you can purchase for the current market value that does need a little renovating. You find that the rent charged should cover all of this over time. But what if our economy or your local economy goes into a recession? Suddenly a lot of people cannot afford that much rent or, worse yet, people are moving away leaving you with a vacant building?

Actually this is not as bad as it may sound. If you have been paying that mortgage for awhile, you might be able to rewrite it for what you have left owing on it for a smaller monthly payment. This might even decrease your monthly costs enough that you can lower the rental charged until things change.

Supposing you bought a unit and now the area is stagnating and you find you cannot increase the rent every two or so years. How about making it more renter friendly or desirable? Is there a spare storage room where you can install a washer and dryer for the convenience of your renters? Personally, we would contract this out to a vending company so they are responsible for keeping the appliances repaired. The contractor gets the coins and you get to charge more for the rental units. Everyone wants to live in a safe area, so can you put a stronger entry door on with improved deadbolts and locks? We even know of one person who actually managed to talk the city bus transportation department to put in a new bus stop just a half block from her building because she could prove that 30% of the people in the area depended on that bus transportation for work.

Perhaps there is an increase in crime in the area causing rents to lower. Can you replace the old entrance with a steel security door and better lighting at the entrance? Can you make your rental units more appealing by cleaning up and landscaping that back yard with a picnic area and flowers? In other words, when times get bad (as they always do), think about what you would want as a renter and see if you can do things that your renters are willing to pay as much as they currently are for or even pay more for.

Also keep in mind that when the economy goes bad you will usually have more people looking for rentals because they cannot afford a house payment thus giving you more potential renters to chose from.

So when you are considering how much to pay for a rental property, you need to look at the current market value to see what your monthly mortgage payment would be. Then, can you charge high enough rent to cover the mortgage and all the other costs. Then, are you interested in just covering costs (for now knowing you will make a profit later) or do you want to make a profit each month starting immediately?

One other thing you need to consider when thinking about getting into rental property is, are you willing to manage the property yourself or do you need to hire someone to do it for you. Obviously, if you hire a rental agent this will be an additional expense for you. You should plan on about $100 to $200 or more a month for this. This agent will find renters for you and take care of any problems that occur. Before going this route, we would suggest you think about it carefully. For one thing, you must be actively involved with the rental property in order to be able to claim all tax deductions. That is, you must be the one who makes the final decision on who to rent to and you must set the criteria. Also remember that you have to keep an eye on agents as they are apt to want to collect their fee and do as little work as possible.

Also, if you are personally doing the interviewing, you will be able to spot things that you do not want to deal with. If you are talking with a potential renter and they are complaining about the place they are leaving, they will be complaining to you next week. Are they trying to pack five kids plus themselves into a two bedroom apartment? You know they will not take proper care of the place.

Personally we have not found it difficult or demanding to take care of the property ourselves. However, we have our own business and, therefore, do not have to worry about working 9 to 5 every day. If you are buying in your area most things such as interviews, repairs, renovations, etc. can be done on weekends.

The secret is to find "good" renters. You need to screen carefully for individuals or families that are willing to pay enough for a nice property and are, therefore, willing to keep it in good condition. Whenever someone lives in a place, it is going to experience wear and tear. You know you will have to repaint everything and there will always be some small repairs and a good cleaning job will be necessary before the next renters can move in. However, normal wear and tear is very different from trashing a place. Create a desirable place to live so that renters will be willing to (and are able to) pay higher rent. Be sure to become familiar with all laws in your area pertaining to non-discrimination.

Have a standard application form for the renters to fill out. Then make sure you spend the time checking their credit history, how long they have been employed, their income, and their previous rentals (do they move around a lot). When you do find suitable renters, make sure you have a rental contract.

Ultimately, you should be looking for a rental property that can command good rental rates (not necessarily "high end") as usually you will have a better class of renters that probably would not destroy your property.

With good renters we have not had a problem with maintenance. A young person might not know what to do when a light bulb goes out. However, they call us directly we tell them that according to their signed contract they are responsible for this so they need to go to a store and buy some spare bulbs. The reactions is always, "Oh, okay." We actually provide a plunger beside each toilet with printed directions how to use it. This saves a lot of phone calls and costs very little. We always have in the contract that we or our representative is allowed to inspect the premises with 24 hours notice as frequently as every 30 days. And we do this! It is important to let people know that you will be checking to make sure they are not trashing the place. After all, kids will be kids even if they are 50 years old! Also, do not do these inspections on a regular basis as they will know when to expect you. You want to see what the average everyday condition is.

Negotiating the price will be the same as in the previous chapter although, as previously mentioned, you will need the income and costs associated with the rental income as this may enable you to bargain better if the rental-versus-expense costs are not too favorable. Also, if the rental unit comes with good tenants that have been there a few years, that could be a higher cost factor favoring the seller. However, if you feel you can improve the property enough to command a higher monthly rental, you can include in the contract that the previous owner will be responsible for paying the current residents to vacate the property (paying off any outstanding lease). Also make sure you receive the original signed leases and the security deposits for these renters if you will be retaining them at that location.

Keep in mind that you should be able to increase the monthly rental by 2% to 3% each year until you get it to the correct rate for the renovations you have done.   You will then have cost of living increases every two to three years of 3% to 5%.   Although rent control is banned in 31 states, other states do mandate what you can charge for rent and when and how much this can be increased. You need to be particularly careful about this in California and the Northeast.

The most important thing when getting into rental units is to have a good contract with the renter. Again, there are standard rental agreements you can buy in any office supply store. Quite often your real estate agent will have some standard contracts. Personally we suggest going to a lawyer to have your own personal contract written up. Make sure it includes the following:

1. List what the renter is responsible for (such as cleaning community hall ways, fixing broken windows, etc.). Also list what you will be responsible for (such as cleaning hall ways or taking care of lawns, etc.).

2. You will need to have spaces for all renters of legal age to sign along with a place for the names of all children that will be living there. Make it clear that no one else will be allowed to live there without passing your scrutiny first.

3. It needs to include a joint and several liability statement. That is, each person living there is responsible for paying the entire rental amount so that if one person leaves the remaining one pays the whole amount.

4. Limit the amount of time any guests can stay in this unit for no more then one week. Otherwise you will end up not knowing who is there or having the actual renter leave and the "guest" having no signed contract with you.

5. Always start with a one year lease in which they must give at least 30 days notice of leaving. At the end of the year, if they have been good tenants, you can offer them a month-to-month rental which will give them more options and encourage them to stay there.

6. The tenants need to understand that if they do not leave on the appointed day, they will be fined $50 per day for each additional day they stay.

7. Make sure you or your agent goes through the property with the renter before they move in to inspect it. If there is any damage, this should be listed in the contract. Also list any of your own property such as appliances with serial numbers and photos in case the renter leaves with your goods.

8. The renter needs to know when the rent is due by and you might consider giving them a discount of 5% if you receive their payment before the due date. To avoid continual late payers, have it written in the contract that if they are late 3 times during the course of the lease, they will be required to vacate immediately.

9. State what the renter will be charged for any bounced checks and if they bounce 3 checks during the course of the lease, they will be required to vacate immediately.

10. They must get your written permission for any changes to the unit such as painting, plantings, etc.

11. They must give the owner access to the unit with 24 hours notice and between the hours of 8:00 am to 8:00 pm. However, no notice will be required in the case of an emergency.

12. Requiring tenant insurance is another way to find good renters that will take care of the property. You should provide a list of recommended insurers.

13. Allowing pets will increase the number of people wanting to rent from you and you can also charge more for this. Put in the contract what size pets are allowed

(have them provide a photo of the pet) and how much each pet will cost per month.

14. You should require a high security deposit (usually one month's rent) plus the first month's rent before they move in. Again, to attract good clients you might want to offer a small annual interest on this amount that they will get back when they leave if everything is in good condition. However, make sure it is stated that the renter is responsible for paying all damages that exceed this deposit.

15. Know what vehicles the renters will have there along with their license plate numbers

16. There will be zero tolerance of drugs, gambling, prostitution or any other illegal activity.

17. The tenant should be responsible for paying all utilities.

18. Any of the renter's possessions not removed by the end of the lease will become yours.

Please check out your local laws concerning rental agreements also although your lawyer should already be familiar with them.

Tax Benefits

There is one more thing you should consider when comparing the price versus your expenses. Interestingly, the thing most people forget about when it comes to rental property is all of the tax benefits. You will be claiming the additional income of the rent but you will have more tax deductions to offset it with (Schedule E is used for claiming rental income and expenses).

1. All property taxes (except for the portion you may be living in) are tax deductible as business expenses.

2. All of the upkeep, maintenance, renovations, etc. are tax deductible business expenses.

3. Anything that is damaged and must be replaced or anything that is stolen and you have to replace is deductible.

4. If you decide to hire a property manager, their fees are deductible.

5. Any travel involved to and from the rental property is deductible.

6. The interest on your mortgage is deductible as well as the insurance coverage.

7. Any legal and accounting costs as well as miscellaneous costs related to the rental are tax deductible.

8. You are also allowed to depreciate the purchase price on your taxes. The law is that 27.5 years is the normal economic life allowed and this is how long you can depreciate it for. However, if it is a business building (no tenants) which we will talk about in the upcoming chapter, you have 39 years to depreciate it in. If it is part tenants and part business, the percentage of each area is apportioned to that particular type of building. If you live in one of the rental units, you cannot depreciate that part of

the property. Yes, we do suggest you hire a good CPA to do your taxes but keep in mind that his fee is also tax deductible.

9. When selling your principal residence (where you reside) you can keep up to $500,000 in profit (married filing jointly) tax free or up to $250,000 is tax free for single people. You must have lived in the house for at least 2 of the past 5 years. You can continue to buy and sell using this tax exemption so long as it is at least two years between.

This law also helps the older home owner. If you retire and now want to downsize your home, you can take the above tax exemption and then use the $500,000 profit to finance a smaller home and even provide the down payments for a couple of rental units for retirement income.

Keep in mind that the IRS and congress are constantly changing tax laws. Therefore, talk to your CPA before you make any final decisions to make sure the above is still accurate.

There are other tax benefits that you might want to consider such as the 20% tax credit for buying and renovating an historic structure, the 10% tax credit for the renovating of non-commercial buildings that were built before 1936 (historic), the 4% tax credit for up to 10 years for low-income housing or the renovation of an older building to create low-income housing. Personally, we like to keep it simple and do not look for properties meeting these criteria. However, some of these might be of interest to you.

Again, keep in mind that you must be actively involved to claim any of these deductions. That is, you set the rental rate, you approve the tenants (even if you hire a property management firm), you make the decisions concerning any improvements, etc. Thus you can claim against the rental income any damages or theft, the depreciation on the property, all maintenance, property taxes, and interest on your mortgage, insurance, etc.

If you made a mistake in buying the property and end up paying out more than the rental brought in for the year, you can claim up to $25,000 in rental property losses against your normal income. However, if your adjusted gross income is more than $100,000 a year, you can only claim 50 cents of every dollar you make over that $100,000. Again, we hire an accountant for this.

You will also have capital gains taxes to pay when you sell the property. Keep in mind that if you own the property for over 12 months, the capital gains tax is currently capped at 15%. If you own it for less then 12 months, you will be taxed at your income rate.

Although you will need to hire a CPA to do your taxes, you should be able to do the necessary bookkeeping yourself (although if you do hire a bookkeeper, that is also tax deductible). You will need to keep track of any improvements, all operating and maintenance costs, and the rental income. This means you must save all receipts pertaining to your property! If you are ever audited by the state or IRS, this will become crucial to your deductions or expenses.

Another thing to keep in mind is that Congress has created an investor tax category called "taxpayers in the real property business". This is basically anyone that deals with real estate that works at least 750 hours per year in it. This entitles you to be exempt from the "passive loss rules" where generally an investor who reports income of more than $100,000 (high-wager earners) from sheltering their earnings from depreciation. If you meet the 750 hours or more per year, you are exempt from the passive loss rules and can use your rental property tax losses to offset any taxable income you may receive from any other types of income such as wages, dividends, interest income, etc. Again, we suggest, especially if you fall into this category, that you should consult a good CPA familiar with rental income. The bank will send you an end-of-year statement showing your total interest paid for the year.

However, you can make rental income on many other properties besides the usual apartments.

FAMILY HOUSE RENTAL

There are a lot of people who would rather live in a house with all of the amenities it includes instead of an apartment. After all, with a house you will usually have more rooms including room enough for an entire family. You will also have a yard to enjoy. And, of course, a house usually means more privacy.

Most people today think of living in a house themselves and then buying rental property for income. However, you can also move up the property ladder by buying a smaller house, fix it up, move to a bigger house (or just another location) and rent out that starter place.

As with buying your own home, you need to be careful. The biggest mistake people make is looking for the exact house **they** want instead of looking for one that will appeal to others also. That is, look for the right location with enough bedrooms (today people want 3 to 4) and baths (at least 2). Although you may find a 2 bedroom with 1 bath house, unless it is at a really attractive price, it will generally command a much smaller rent and also be more difficult to find a renter.

In order to have potential people to rent this house, you need to have certain things in a fairly close area. That is, you could own a farm house miles out in the country because that is where **you** wanted to live. However, how many people will want to drive that far between home and their job. So, consider the following:

1. Are there jobs within 20 miles of this house?
2. Are there schools within 2 miles?
3. Are there stores within 2 miles?
4. Is there public transportation available?
5. If in the country, are water, sewer and utilities available and in good condition? Or do you need to provide a new well and septic system?

Who rents a whole house instead of an apartment? People with families who are moving into the area may decide to rent a house (large enough for the whole family) until they decide where to buy a home. Some families cannot get the down payment together in order to buy a house of their own. Young people starting out would rather rent then buy a house or condo realizing that they will probably be moving for career advancement in the near future. A lot of younger people prefer the quiet of a house rather than an apartment. College students will often rent a house together. Retired people sometimes prefer renting instead of owning a house so they are not tied down to one place or they will down size to a smaller house.

How does renting out your first house help you? If you have already lived in this house for several years, chances are you have already built equity in it. This means you can borrow against that equity for the down payment on your next home. But rather than sell the first property, why not rent it out for the additional income.

Again, we are back to making sure you can make a profit from this property. If you are still using the original mortgage you got on the property, see if you can refinance it in order to bring your out-of-pocket costs down. That is, it might be difficult to rent a house for $2,000 a month (depending on your area) but, by refinancing, you might be able to bring that monthly rental down to $1,200 a month making it much more affordable for you. Also, interest rates may be down from when you originally purchased the house. You may have purchased it at an 8% rate but the current rate is 6%. Just this in itself would save you about $150 or more per month in lower payments on a 30 year loan. Keep in mind, we are *not* talking about making it more affordable for the renter! You want to maximize the rental and lower your monthly costs to create more profit.

One of the biggest mistakes owners make when renting out any property is creating a low monthly rental in order to attract renters. A low price will attract renters alright, but probably the wrong kind. After spending your time and money to fix a place up you do not want to see renters immediately trash it. Therefore, keep the rent as high as your area will bear. You need to attract renters who are willing to pay a premium price for a nice place. These are the ones who will keep the place up because that is what they want to live in. However, by refinancing your mortgage to a lower price, you can make a bigger profit from what you charge the renter and/or in hard times you will have a lower monthly cost.

Again, you must make enough in rental income to cover the monthly mortgage payment, the taxes, insurance, and maintenance costs. We prefer to have the contract cover the renter paying the utilities. Thus anything over these costs is your profit.

You can and will be increasing the rental amount over time also. For instance, you may consider renting the property furnished for a higher rent (particularly if you want to replace your own home's furnishings anyway). Also remember that you should be increasing the rental two to three percent each year to cover the normal increase in the cost of living.

Remember that so long as you keep this property in excellent condition, it will continue to appreciate in value and you will be paying off more and more of the mortgage. Yes, this means more profit for you in the future. However, as with everything in life, the monthly rental will slowly increase over the years along with the cost of living. Therefore, you are paying less and less but making more and more.

However, for the sake of argument, let's say you bought a house for $300,000. You supplied a down payment of $60,000. You find the monthly rental income is just covering the mortgage payment and other costs with no profit left over. However, as it is covering costs you decide to hold onto the house for 20 years and then sell it. But, after 20 years you find that property values are still the same in your area so you can only get $300,000 for it (highly unlikely though). Does this mean you lost money on this deal? No, because you only paid $60,000 out of your own pocket with everything else being paid by the rent money. Of course, after 20 years there usually would have been some appreciation no matter how bad the situation was, but we wanted to point this out to you.

We just referred to keeping this property in excellent condition. This means you should take care of the lawns and outdoor areas rather than expecting the renter to do this (you can certainly hire someone for this). This way you will know that at least the outside is being well taken care of. However, it also gives you an opportunity to keep a closer eye on the place.

People trash rental property when they know they can get away with it. Therefore, make sure you always have in the rental agreement a clause allowing you access to the house (or apartment or whatever you are renting) at any time with 24 hours notice. And then, most importantly, follow through on this at least twice a year but preferably more often. We have local rentals that we go to them to collect the monthly rental. The renter thinks this is a nice thing we do for them so they don't have to bother going somewhere to make the payment. However, it allows us to keep an eye on the place as most people will leave the door open or even invite you in while they go for their check book. Make sure you do not set up a regular schedule of visitations so that the renters will be pressed to keep everything in order not knowing when to expect a visit from the owner. Unfortunately, we have found that most rental agencies say they will inspect like this, but we have found that they usually do no inspections at all.

We personally feel it is very important that you take care of the rental yourself for several reasons. First of all, why pay someone else when you can keep that rental agency fee in your own pocket? Second, if you do the interviewing yourself, you can keep control of who is going to rent from you. Keep in mind that a rental agency just has to have someone in there at the price you want. So long as the renter can pass a credit check, the agency does not care whether the renter seems to be a responsible person or not. Third, by staying hands on, you can keep an eye on what is happening. If you see problems developing, you need to talk to the renters quickly before the problem gets out of control. This means letting them know that they have 30 days in which to get the place back into its original order (make sure you can provide photos of the original condition) or you will start the eviction process. Fourth, you need to have this hands-on approach in order to make sure you are able to receive the proper tax deductions for business purposes.

Obviously, you do not have to stop at living in one house while renting out your old house. You can keep climbing the property ladder (or moving sideways if you prefer) until you have enough rental houses to live comfortably from or you can keep it small with just one or two rentals as it is all up to you.

Also, do not make any improvements on the house while you live there are too far out. What we are saying is, you might want to live in a tropical garden for your master bedroom with wildly colored wallpaper and exotic looking fixtures. This is fine for you while you live there but can be a big hindrance when either selling or renting the house out later. You would have to find someone that likes that hula skirt around the wall or you will have to renovate it to be more conventional.

However, a family house is certainly not the only property you can earn rental from. Do you like taking vacations?

VACATION PROPERTY RENTAL

Buying vacation property and then renting it out in order to make it pay for its self has been very popular since the 1950's. Most people have a particular area that they love to visit every year such as spending a week at the ocean or up in the mountains by the lake. Some people prefer areas that meet their hobby requirements such as the mountains for skiing or the southern oceans for scuba diving. Some want a place close to their family so they can visit once a year but still have their own space. And some people (like us) like to go to different places each year.

You should also be forewarned that vacation rental property is probably the most risky as you have so many variables such as just how desirable is the location and how good or bad the economy is. Most vacation rentals are also seasonal and are simply impractical or even impossible to rent out for the entire year. For instance, a vacation home on the coast of Maine is fine during the summer months but what about during the winter when it is 10° below zero outside?

In order to get the tax deductions you must have the property rented out more than 15 days each year and you cannot use it for your own vacation more than 10% of the days it is rented out.

Buying vacation property can take care of all of these for you or it can become a nightmare. You don't want a huge mortgage that you plan on paying by rental income and then find out no one is interested in your personal vacation spot. The secret is to do your research. For instance, surveys show that the best vacation spots (most people want to go to that area) are:

1. Ocean locations
2. Lake or river locations
3. Mountain locations
4. Southern locations (for snowbirds)
5. Dessert locations

Obviously some of these can be combined into one property such as the coastal mountains of the west coast that are within an easy drive to the ocean or a mountain location right on a lake. Also keep in mind that decorating that vacation home appropriately for its location (an ocean cottage with ocean blues and sand colors with seashells around and striped canvas furniture or a mountain home with lots of raw wood and plaids) will fetch a higher rental than a blah interior.

You need to consider where your family likes to vacation but keep in mind those areas that will be easier to rent out when you are not there. For instance, the southern areas are very popular in the winter when northerners want the warmth but practically impossible to rent out in the summer when the average temperature is in the 90's with 90% humidity. Our son, David, loves Phoenix and the 115° "dry" heat in the summer, but most people do not. A place in the mountains is fine in the winter if there are good skiing areas nearby and good in the summer if there is a lake or river for water sports. In other words, most vacation spots are not good year round.

When considering a vacation rental property, you need to realize that you probably will not make any profit from it. That is, you will use it a few days or weeks each year and you may be able to rent it out for a few weeks or a couple of months (especially if you can build up repeat business). However, surveys show that the majority of vacation rentals do not pay for themselves. Therefore, this is only for those who simply want some help paying for that get away realizing the rental will not cover everything.

You also need to consider that it will not be all play and no work. A vacation home is still another home which means upkeep. Do you want to spend your time off mowing a lawn? If not, you want something more primitive such as a cottage under trees (where no grass will grow). You cannot count on the rental income either as vacationing is very affected by our economic circumstances. During a recession you may not be able to rent it out making it even more difficult to meet the monthly mortgage payment.

Also, if it is in a very desirable vacation area such as near where we live in Lake Tahoe, property is very expensive so the owner's have voted to limit the number of new buildings keeping the number of rentals very limited. Because there are so few rentals, these are usually much easier to keep filled.

Although we are not into this type of rental ourselves, we have been told by friends who are that vacation renters are much more demanding than apartment or house renters. They are paying their hard-earned money for a one or two week vacation and they expect it to be perfect. So make sure everything is working correctly and in good repair.

Vacation rentals also mean you will need to supply all furnishings and usually bedding, linens, etc. People expect a vacation rental to be furnished in an appropriate style (mountain area will be rustic, seashore area will have light summer colors, etc.)

There is also another type of rental property that we have used. If you like going to different spots, an RV might be the right thing for you. It's easy to go wherever you want whether ocean, mountains, or dessert as there are campgrounds everywhere. If the RV is totally self-contained (it has heat, water, bathroom), it is considered a second home with the appropriate tax deductions. And, yes, you can rent it out to help pay for the unit. For instance, a reasonable Class C RV (this is a motorized motorhome on a cutaway van chassis) might cost you $85,000 (plus taxes and licensing, insurance, and maintenance) and cost you about $650 a month. Keep in mind that this can be financed for as long as a 15 year mortgage (for a second home) at current rates. Personally, we prefer to rent to people we know well and believe they will not abuse it and, therefore, only charge $75 a day. Obviously, if someone rented at this rate for a two week trip (they pay all gas costs), you would more than cover the mortgage payment, although not the other miscellaneous costs. However, the prevailing rate in our area for a Class C Motorhome is $1,100 to $1,400 per week and 15 cents to 25 cents per mile over the 100 miles allowed per day.

Keep in mind that this type of rental requires that you spend some time with the client showing them how things operate and what to handle things. Unfortunately, you can end up with a lot of clean up when it is returned because people make mistakes or do not remember that you said to always dump the black holding tank (sewage) before the gray one (sink and shower water). You RVer's will know what we mean. You want to make sure they also have vehicle insurance that will pay you if they have an accident or else provide additional insurance for this yourself (which you will charge them for).

As with any real estate, you should be taking a security deposit up front until the unit is returned and you can inspect the RV.

Another self-contained vehicle is a boat (with water and bathroom) which is also considered a second home and can also be rented out. Boats are not our cup of tea as you are restricted to a certain body of water unless you want to pay to have it hauled to another area. Again, you will have to plan on that extra time to acquaint the renters with how to operate everything. You will also have to check their insurance and do everything else as mentioned above for an RV rental.

As with any property, you want to be choosey as to whom you rent to. Are these people well dressed and driving a nice car or do they look like they live in their car? Also, keep the rental high enough to rule out those just looking for a place to stay. Although a boat large enough to be considered a second home is somewhat tied down to a certain area, an RV can go anywhere. Therefore, you have a better chance of renting both winter and summer with an RV.

Some considerations with vacation rentals is to make sure all fees are paid up front along with a hefty deposit in case of problems. Again, if you find someone to rent from you who is conscientious, try to get them as repeat customers by offering special off-season deals or lower prices for a longer rental period. If you know these people take care of things, it is worth offering them a special price next year.

However, we stress making money from property in this book. So will you make anything from vacation rental property? You will probably not be able to cover all of your costs, however, keep in mind that with actual property (not boats or RVs) you can build equity in the value of that property over time while boats and RVs depreciate over time. But perhaps we should get back to actually making money from your real estate investment. One of the best and worst ways is through commercial property rental.

COMMERCIAL PROPERTY RENTAL

Yes, commercial property is the best and the worst way to make money. It is the best in that commercial property can be rented out at much higher rates. Also, once a business is in a location, they usually want to stay there for a long time. The worst part is when that renter leaves. Commercial property can stay vacant for months or even years while you are trying to find another business to locate there.

However, the question remains, is commercial property the right investment for you. Are you willing to put a lot more time and money into your investment? That is, good commercial real estate is difficult to find as most such places are already owned. If you happen to find someone trying to sell a strip mall, there is probably a good reason such as they are losing money on it. These owners are not willing to part with such property very often and, when they do decide to, they want to get a very good profit from their sale. In other words, even if you can afford to buy it, it could take years before you are making a profit from the rental.

The most affordable way to get into commercial real estate is to look for a house that can be renovated into office space. For instance, that little town outside of the city you live in could have old (as in very large) houses in what is now the downtown area of that town. In the 1800's, we had a lot of small towns spring up with the residents building on the outskirts or just off "Main Street". As the population grew, the downtown area grew and now encompasses these older homes. The problem is, most of these have already been purchased so you may have a long search for any more of them. Another problem is, because they are old buildings, they could entail a lot more expense in order to convert them. However, as mentioned before, there are tax breaks for converting renovating very old buildings. Check with your CPA before counting on that business deduction though.

The other problem is the money involved. To convert a home into office space is very costly and usually much more difficult then fixing up an older home that will be for a family's use. Also, usually the new business tenant will want you, the owner, to do the renovating for their particular needs. That is, is there going to be a dentist's office on the first floor and that he has a particular floor plan he wants created. He will need special equipment that might be very heavy so the floor must be strong enough to support it. Also, the electrical system will need to be upgraded for that x-ray machine, etc. These are just a few of the potentially expensive modifications you might need to make.

What you are looking for is a small town near a larger city (that is attracting suburbanites) with an old downtown area. As our population booms, people are moving further away from the cities but still commuting in to work. In just the past 15 years, we have seen towns surrounding Sacramento that were just about deserted spring back to life with new people moving in (for cheaper housing and more affordable living) that need these small office businesses.

Keep in mind that there are real estate agents who specialize in business properties. However, if you let them know what you are trying to do, they can be very helpful in watching for such buildings.

You will have to carefully research and test out the waters to see if you can get this house rezoned for business. This explains why so many businessmen are on town planning boards. If you cannot get the rezoning, then there is no need to even consider this property.

The financing is more difficult to get in that we are talking about a lot more money between the purchasing and the renovating. This means a higher down payment but, also, you will be building more equity if the market holds up. By that we mean that a small town that is growing can also go the other way. A lot is dependent on whether that small town can provide the services, schools, and infrastructure that people need to live comfortably. It doesn't hurt to sit on a town council meeting to see what is going on. Talk with some of these council people to see if they want their town to grow or are they trying to keep it a small town.

Assuming you find a good property and do the renovation to turn it into a nice clean "officey" looking interior, you still need to find tenants. This can be very time consuming and costly in itself with the advertising involved. However, how long can you keep paying the mortgage until you have businesses in those offices?

Renting commercial property is for those of you who are willing to put a lot more time and money into the project realizing that the risks are also higher. You will definitely need to get a lawyer involved for the lease contracts and their knowledge of commercial rental situations and local and state laws. You will need to find a real estate broker who specializes in commercial property also. If you still question how risky this could possibly be, check out some local small commercial buildings to see what percentage of the space is leased and what percentage is looking to be filled. You could even pretend to be looking for an office space to find this out and perhaps, in the course of conversation, you can find out how long this place has been vacant (or you may be able to tell from the dust).

Another form of rental property that could help you with this situation is mixed commercial and residential rentals.

MIXED COMMERCIAL AND APARTMENT RENTALS

Something that could help you in several ways is to consider making the old house a mixed commercial and apartment building. That is, the first floor could be a small restaurant or specialty store while the upstairs is turned into apartments. This means you could live in one of the apartments while working on the renovating of the upstairs yourself and it is easier to rent out apartments then commercial space. Thus you would at least have some rental income produced from the upstairs while waiting to fill the downstairs.

However, this also comes with problems such as is there sufficient parking for this use, does it meet the zoning regulations, can the building be brought back to code compliance? The biggest problem with this today is that those small restaurants and specialty stores have a tendency to not succeed and within a year or two you are left with an empty space and trying to find another business renter. This is another instance where your hands-on involvement can really help. What can you do to help this small business become successful? Can you help with special promotions or distribute flyers with introductory coupons for them? What can you do to make sure their entrance is very visible and attractive? Unfortunately, most small business owners may know a lot about their business but very little about marketing that business. This is where it behooves you to help them out.

However, this can also create more expense for you concerning your apartment renters. No one likes a noisy home. Is there someway to block the noise a kitchen might make to keep the apartment above it nice and quiet? If there is noise up till say 10 o'clock each night, can you work out a deal with the restaurant wherein your tenants get big discounts for eating there? Usually specialty stores on the first floor do not create the same amount of noise.

Again, because you are talking about a larger property, you are talking more financing with a relatively larger down payment. Remodeling will be involved but, if you are willing to do the apartments yourself, you can help keep these costs down. Zoning is all important. If you cannot get the zoning for a commercial business, then you are left with a building that can only be sold as a home. However, the reward is that you will always have some income from the apartments.

There are other ways to invest in real estate, some that don't even take any time on your part, that we do not personally recommend.

OTHER FORMS OF PROPERTY INVESTMENT

As with any type of investing, we will not go into anything that we feel is so risky that even Eric would never invest in such a thing. However, we feel obligated to mention these other forms of real estate investing.

Real Estate Investment Trusts (REITs for short) are usually publicly traded mutual funds that specialize in just real estate. However, there are a lot of different kinds of REITs. For instance, if at least 95% of the earnings from the trust is passed on to the shareholders as dividends, then your investment is tax free. However, most REITs are other investors looking for money and will keep most of the profit for themselves.

There are rental REITs wherein you gain equity from the rent from this real estate. There are also mortgage REITs wherein you get income from the interest charged on the mortgages. There are also a combination of these two wherein you gain equity and income.

They are traded on a daily basis meaning you must be willing to watch closely for the right time to get out of it. Also, you have no control over these as you do with your own property. More importantly though is who is behind them. If it was created by a developer or contractor, then it might be all speculation meaning that they could have to sell property at a loss or even go bankrupt meaning you would lose everything.

Another way to invest in real estate is to buy undeveloped land. This can sometimes be very easy to find as more and more farmers cannot make a decent living or their children do not want to carry on the family farm so the owners want to sell their large holding of land and retire. It can also be much harder to find in an urban setting. Here in Sacramento there was a great deal of vacant land just 5 years ago. Today, with our growth, there is very little undeveloped vacant land unless you are willing to drive 15 miles outside the city. However, do to the decreasing availability of land, more and more people are willing to commute further distances.

The problem comes in selling the land. Trying to develop it yourself would be extremely costly and time consuming as this is a full time business. So unless you are worth millions, you will need to hold onto this land, paying the mortgage meanwhile as there will be no rental income, until it has appreciated in value enough to interest a developer.

This is particularly dangerous today with the new laws being developed for eminent domain. That is, we have seen right in our area, homes being taken away from the owners in order to develop something "for the good of the general public" such as a shopping mall or business center. And then the developer has to get approval for the use they want to put it to and it must pass environmental laws. Unfortunately, the owners usually do not receive the current value of their property and end up having to start over buying whatever house they can afford. Personally, we are wondering what ever happened to "freedom" in this country.

By the way, have you ever wondered why there are so many storage businesses popping up everywhere? This is raw land that a speculator has bought and, rather than let it just sit there for years, they build storage units to pay for the mortgage costs. Then in three to ten years as things change and people are looking for more homes, they will tear down the storage facility and build homes on the land to sell.

You might also have noticed that we did not talk about buying and selling of condos or coops. The record over the past 35+ years (condos developed in this country around 1960) for these types of properties has not been good. It is difficult for a condo or coop to appreciate because, the fact remains, Americans like living in their own house. We have also seen situations wherein the owners of the building will change apartments into condos in order to get out of the rental business and get the money from actually selling the space. However, the person buying that space usually loses in that they are lucky to get what they paid for it at a later date. We have also seen apartments switched to condos (for the above reasons) only to see it switched back to apartments because there is a glut of condos on the market.

Both the condos and the coops are much more complex to handle. For instance, with a condo there is common space that must be taken care of which means monthly maintenance fees and you are only buying the space enclosed by the walls but not the walls themselves. Again, most Americans do not care for this. With a coop you don't own anything but are rather leasing the space with the right to sell that space to someone else.

Yes, you can make money with these but you have a large risk of losing also. We prefer to invest in things that are relatively safe.

BACK TO MAKING MONEY

What this all boils down to is that you can make excellent money in real estate if you understand what is necessary including your time, your labor, and your money. You need to understand the good potentials of investing in real estate but you also need to understand the pitfalls.

You will make more profit if you are willing to do the work yourself. Anything you need hired is going to take away from your profits. Personally, we get a great feeling of accomplishment from fixing a place up but you may not like the labor involved.

We admit we are currently more partial to rental property, however, we intend to eventually sell some of it to take care of things in our older years. If you are younger, you may be looking to buy and sell relatively quickly in order to get into a better home than you could otherwise afford.

Always keep in mind that, contrary to the ads, this is work and not that easy. It is not like investing in safe secure stock and sitting back to let it grow. Real estate is a riskier investment and, if not done correctly, could be extremely risky for you.

Even if you decide not to get into real estate investing, you will probably still buy your own home some day. Your home will probably be the biggest investment you ever make so think about how you can make it grow in value for you. If you already have bought your home, it is never too late to renovate in order to increase its value. This increased value will help you when you do decide someday to sell it. Or, if you live in it till the day you don't need a home any more, you can still use this increased value for a reverse mortgage when you retire.

As with all of our previous books, if you have any questions or want another's opinion (for what it is worth), feel free to contact us at ELPBooks@aol.com. And let us hear how you do with your investing!

Books by Bobbie and Eric Christensen

Building Your Financial Portfolio On $25 A Month, 4th Edition ($15.95)

Adding To Your Financial Portfolio, 2nd Edition ($15.95)

Top 50 Best Stock Investments, 3rd Edition ($19.95)

Building Your Debt-Free Life ($14.95)

Retirement Planning For Everyone ($12.95)

Smart Real Estate Investing ($15.95)

Common Sense Portfolio newsletter ($26-1 yr, $47-2 yrs)

Books by Bobbie Christensen

Building Your Dream Life: Career, Sex & Leisure, 2nd Edition ($14.95)

The Banker Chronicles, a mystery ($14.95)

Writing, Publishing & Marketing Your 1st Book (or 7th) On A Shoe-String Budget ($15.95)

Books by Eric Christensen
Fly Fishing For Fun ($15.95)

All orders add $4 for shipping and handling.

To order, call 1-800-929-7889 (Mastercard & Visa accepted)
Or mail check or money order to:
BooksAmerica, PO Box 232233, Sacramento, CA 95823
Or order online at www.BooksAmerica.com
Prices guaranteed through 12/06